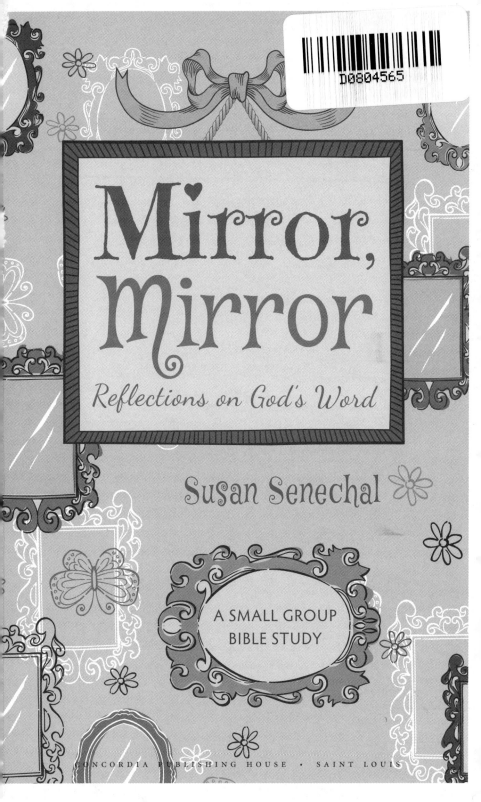

Mirror, Mirror

Reflections on God's Word

Susan Senechal

A SMALL GROUP
BIBLE STUDY

CONCORDIA PUBLISHING HOUSE • SAINT LOUIS

To Karen and Amy, who reflect God's love to me as we
struggle through life together, and in memory of my dad,
Arnold Rathje, who mirrored Christ to everyone he met. "For we
are [God's] workmanship, created in Christ Jesus for good works,
which God prepared beforehand, that we should walk in them"
(Ephesians 2:10). —Susan

Copyright © 2015 Concordia Publishing House
3558 S. Jefferson Avenue, St. Louis, MO 63118-3968
1-800-325-3040 • www.cph.org

Unless otherwise indicated, all Scripture quotations are from the ESV Bible®
(The Holy Bible, English Standard Version®), copyright © 2001 by Crossway Bibles,
a publishing ministry of Good News Publishers. Used by permission. All rights
reserved.

Quotations marked KJV are from the King James or Authorized Version of the Bible.

Scripture quotations marked NIV are taken from the Holy Bible, NEW INTERNA-
TIONAL VERSION®, NIV®. Copyright © 1973, 1978, 1984, 2011 by Biblica, Inc.®
Used by permission of Zondervan. All rights reserved.

All italics in Bible passages added by author for emphasis.

Cover and interior art: © iStockphoto.com; © Shutterstock, Inc.

Manufactured in the United States of America

1 2 3 4 5 6 7 8 9 10   24 23 22 21 20 19 18 17 16 15

TABLE OF CONTENTS

Introduction

Introduction

Mirror Message

"We are [God's] workmanship." Ephesians 2:10a

I don't like what I see when I look in the mirror. Many women I know don't either. For there we may see wrinkles and graying hair, crow's-feet and liver spots, sags and bags, and . . . how did that two-inch chin hair get there? We lament our muffin top or our bony elbows. Our breasts are never the right size. When we look in the mirror, we see wouldas and couldas and shouldas—and regrets aplenty. We don't like what our reflection says about where we've been and where we're going, so we try to cover what we see with the right makeup and the perfect new outfit. And if we're still not happy, we try not to look in the mirror at all. But consider this: we're seeing our reflections as in a fun house mirror—warped and distorted.

The truth is that we don't see ourselves the way God sees us. He is our Creator and Redeemer. God sees us through the filter of the cross, in the reflection of His Son, with the eyes of love. This study will help us learn to see ourselves this way as well. An image in a piece of glass doesn't reflect who we are in Christ. Looking instead at the person God created us to be will help us form a clearer vision of who we truly are. And God gives us more than a mirror to see that—He gives us His Word.

The sessions in Mirror, Mirror focus on looking at ourselves as God sees us. The One who created us knows us intimately; He knows the name He has given us, and He knows the plans He has for us. He has called us into His family and has a job for each of us there. He sees our true beauty even when we see only regrets. And He has a plan for even our most damaged past. He is the one who says to each of us, "I have loved you with an everlasting love; therefore I have continued My faithfulness to you" (Jeremiah 31:3).

Designed as a women's small group study, Mirror, Mirror not only delves into the Bible, it also asks you to make personal applications to your own life. Sessions are designed to provide a comfortable place where you can gather with other women and discover who you are according to the truth of God's Word.

Each session includes a **Mirror Message**, a Bible passage to help you remember who you are in Christ, and thought-provoking questions to help you apply the passage to your own life. My hope is that each of you would place these verses on your mirror as daily (and even hourly) reminders throughout the sessions. And my prayer is that by the end of the study, each of you would know how deeply loved and beautiful you are in Christ.

The author

SESSION ONE

KNOWING
THE PERSON
YOU SEE IN THE
MIRROR

MIRROR MESSAGE

"Fear not, for I have redeemed you; I have called you
by name, you are Mine." Isaiah 43:1

One of the first people I see every day when I get up is . . .
myself. Shortly after rising, I'm sure to get a peek at myself
in the mirror, whether I want to or not. And I always know the
name of the person I see . . . Susan Marie. Sometimes, however,
that's not what I call her, at least in my head. I might call her
"Grumpy," or "Sleepy," or "Bashful," or even . . . "Ugly." Sometimes I get her name wrong.

I am horrible with names. One of the first things I tell new
ladies in my Bible study class is that if I don't remember their
name, it's not because I don't care about them. Really. I come

by it genetically. Growing up the fourth of five children, and the third girl, my dad often called me "CinLinSue" (Cindy, Linda, Susan) or, on a bad day, "DaCinLinSue" (our brother David was the oldest). When my future husband came to my parent's home for Christmas the first time, he was called David, Jeff (my brother-in-law), and Mike (my cousin's husband) more often than he was called Mark (his given name). We joke that we should wear nametags so my family can get the names right.

But the story I use to prove to my new Bible study friends that it's not them, it's me, is the one about something that took place a few months after I got engaged. I was invited to a friend's wedding, which took place in a community where I used to teach. Of course, I took my soon-to-be husband, although he knew no one else who would be there. The ceremony was lovely, and after it was over, I was ready to say hello to some friends. The first one was sitting just a couple of rows behind us. As we were leaving the church, I said, "Hi, Donna. How are you?" (Donna's name has been changed to protect the innocent . . . or because I have forgotten her real name). And then, by way of introduction, I added, "This is my fiancé, Tim." My fiancé stuck out his hand toward hers and said, "Nice to meet you, Donna. My name is Mark." That's right, I *got my fiancé's name wrong*. No, it wasn't a Freudian slip; Tim was actually the groom. It's just that I was working so hard to remember this woman's name that I forgot Mark's. Ouch. But he's good-natured about it, and a few months later I did remember to say, "I, Susan, take you, Mark. . . ."

How about you? Are you good with names? Do you have any tips to share about how you do it? If so, I'm all ears.

Do you know what your name means? Did you perhaps choose the names for your children because of their meanings?

Mark and I did. After a long wait through the adoption process, we named our son Matthew, as we knew that surely it was only by a "gift of God" that we welcomed him into our family. When the time came to adopt our second child, a girl, I chose the name Brianna because I liked the name, although my husband wasn't sold on it. On the day we went to meet her birthmother, in the seventh month of her pregnancy, we arrived at the adoption agency only to find out that she was in the hospital in premature labor. We spent the day praying for the child who might soon be ours, and when my husband discovered that *Brianna* means "strong," he knew we had a name by which to call our child, who would have to be strong to survive if born that early. Praise God the contractions were stopped, and Brianna was born right on time two months later. Little did we know that God would answer our prayers for a strong daughter by making her strong-*willed* as well.

I'm not sure my parents looked up names in a book before naming me, but in recent years I have found their choice fascinating. According to baby name books that I've consulted, *Susan* means "like a lily." I had always thought that was a stupid meaning. After all, what does it mean to be "like a lily"? Then one day in Bible study, we read Luke 12:27–31 and suddenly it became clear to me. "Consider the lilies . . . do not seek what you are to eat and what you are to drink, nor be worried." What an apt description of me, the anti-worrier. And what an appropriate name.

1. Take a moment to look up your name in a baby name book. There are also baby name sources online. Can you see a way in which your name describes you? If yes, share it.

In biblical times, name was associated with character: what a person was called was what a person was. Naming something or someone implied dominion or ownership. Names had significance. I'm not sure that's so true today. I'm not sure what "Moon Unit" means or what is the significance of "Snookie." But in the beginning, right from Genesis 1, names had meaning. In Genesis 1:26, we read "Then God said, 'Let us make *man* in our image." The Hebrew word is *adam*. That's right, Adam means "man." Cain means "brought forth," and his brother's name, Abel, means "meaningless, empty." With a name that reminds me of the British throne's "an heir and a spare," little could Eve have known the shortness and emptiness of her second son's life.

2. When Rebekah's second son was born (Genesis 25:26), what was he named?

The name means literally "he grasped the heel," but figuratively in Hebrew it meant "deceiver." Think about the contemporary idiom "You're pulling my leg." A quick glance at Genesis 27 will give you just one example of Jacob's name ringing true to his character.

So, name means character. What you are called is who you are.

Now read Isaiah 43:1. Notice the words "He who *created* you, O Jacob." The Hebrew word is *bara*. It is first used in the Bible in Genesis 1:1, "In the beginning, God. . . ." The Hebrew word for "create" is used only of divine, never of human, activity. When God is speaking to His people in Isaiah 43:1, He reminds them that He has a unique and special claim on them as their Creator. He reminds us that He is our Creator as well.

• • •

Read the next line: "He who *formed* you, O Israel." The Hebrew word is *yatsar*. (The first use of this word is in Genesis 2:7.) Y*atsar* means "to squeeze or mold into form (like pottery); to determine, form, fashion, shape, and purpose." God created you (from nothing), formed you, molded you, shaped you, and determined your purpose, right from the beginning.

The next part of Isaiah 43:1 reads, *"Fear not."* Do you recall from your elementary school days what kind of sentence this is? If you said "imperative," you are correct. "Fear not!" It's a command, kind of like "Thou shalt not fear." No matter what the situation looks like, no matter what circumstance you are facing, do not be afraid.

Is there something you are facing right now that makes this command difficult? If you feel comfortable, share it with your group. If you're not comfortable sharing it with others, just share it right now with God in a quick prayer. It can be this simple: "God, I'm having trouble remembering Your command to fear not. Help me to trust in You."

Through the prophet Isaiah, God now continues the sentence: "I have redeemed you."

I love a good coupon—fifty cents or a dollar at the grocery store, a coupon for a discount at dinner (my kids say we won't even go out if we don't have a coupon; they call us cheap). But have you ever looked at the bottom of a coupon? Most say "not redeemable for cash" or "cash value 1/100 of a cent." Coupons are worthless unless redeemed properly.

3. In the Bible, a "redeemer" (often called "kinsman-redeemer" because this person was a relative) is someone who bought an unfortunate relative out of slavery or paid a debt. The kinsman-redeemer rescued him or her by paying the slave price or the debt he or she could not pay. When God calls Himself our Redeemer in this verse, it looks forward to the price He would pay on the cross. As New Testament believers, we can look back on it. What are we told in 1 Peter 1:18–19?

The NIV translation uses the word "redeemed," while the ESV says "ransomed." Bought with a price, we are no longer trapped, helpless, worthless, hopeless in our sinful state, but dearly loved and freed children of God.

4a. The next line of the verse reads "summoned" in the NIV, but I prefer the ESV version: "I have called you by name." The same Hebrew word is used in Exodus 31:2 and in Isaiah 45:3–4. In each of those passages, what meaning is implied by the word translated "called" or "summoned" in Isaiah 43:1?

God "calls me by name." He doesn't say, "Hey you, over there, come here." Unlike my dad, He doesn't run down a list of names until He gets to the right one. He chose me and you specifically, invited us into His presence, brought us into His family. He does not summon us in the legal sense of the word, but as the first definition in my dictionary explains, "to call upon to do something specified."

● ● ●

Summon is from the Latin word *summonere*, which means "to remind." God calls me by name and reminds me that I am His, as Isaiah 43:1 continues, "I have called you by name, you are Mine."

    b. We are God's twice over because He is our Creator and our Redeemer. What do we learn about this choosing, this calling, in Deuteronomy 7:6–8?

We are chosen simply because God loved us and chose to call us. We are His treasured possession.

    5a. Some of us, however, may have names we don't like. We have been called hurtful names by a bully at school or work, a parent, a spouse, or even ourselves when we look in the mirror: fat, skinny, useless, worthless, unloved. What did Sarah call herself in Genesis 18:11–12?

    b. What does Gideon call himself in Judges 6:15?

    c. What does God call Gideon in Judges 6:12?

What we have been named or called, or how we see ourselves, is not necessarily who we are. This is not a contradiction of what I said earlier about naming conventions in biblical times because God doesn't just call us by our given name—He renames us. Read Isaiah 62:2–4.

● ● ●

As God restores His people unto Himself, He gives them a new name. The new name reflects a new status. Notice the name changes in verse 4: From Forsaken to Hephzibah, which means "My Delight is in Her"; from Desolate to Beulah, which means "married." God's new names for us reflect our new status in Him and His delight in us. The new name, then, is one through which God bestows on us honor, authority, and character.

And now look again at the end of Isaiah 62:2: "that the mouth of the LORD will give." The Hebrew word for "mouth" is *peh*. It means "mouth, as a means of blowing." Blowing reminds me of breath, and breath reminds me of the Holy Spirit. Take a look at Genesis 1:2. Write the second half of the verse here:

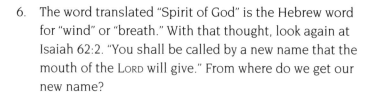

6. The word translated "Spirit of God" is the Hebrew word for "wind" or "breath." With that thought, look again at Isaiah 62:2. "You shall be called by a new name that the mouth of the LORD will give." From where do we get our new name?

In fact, it is as we are filled with the Spirit in Holy Baptism that we receive our new identity.

• • •

7. So, God doesn't just name us, He renames us. And really, as the Creator, He is the only one with the right to name. Remember, in biblical times, to name something implied dominion and ownership. What did God tell Adam in Genesis 2:19?

Let's take a look at the way God renames some of His people. Most of the names and "renames" will be given as part of the text in your Bible or a footnote on the verse.

In Genesis 17:5–6, Abram is renamed Abraham, which means "exalted father." When I think of an exalted father, I think of cultures that honor and esteem a man who has lived many years. On a trip I took to Kenya, I saw that everyone who entered a room bowed their head to a man simply because of his longevity. On the one hand, a man may have been called "exalted father" even if his offspring had been few. On the other, "father of a multitude of nations" can mean only numerous offspring, as Abraham is told in verse 5.

In Genesis 32:26–28, Jacob, whose name meant _____, is renamed Israel, which means _____. In this passage, Jacob has just spent the night struggling, or wrestling, with God. I don't know much about wrestling, but I do know that you cannot wrestle someone from across the room. It's a contact sport. Hand to hand. Body to body. When God renames Jacob Israel, He says, "You have gotten close to Me." We, too, may be renamed by God when we wrestle with Him, when we go through a tough battle and prevail, when we draw near to Him.

8. Can you name a time when you wrestled with God? Was this a time when He "renamed" you and called you "Beloved, Blessed, Chosen"? If you like, talk about this experience with your group, or simply make a note of it here.

9a. What are we told in Psalm 73:28?

In Matthew 16:17–18, Jesus calls Simon *Peter*, which sounds like the Greek word for rock. And in Acts 13:9, Saul (whose name means "asked of God") is called *Paul*, which means "little" and emphasizes his humility and weakness in Christ. I can't help but think that this name change is part of the story behind 2 Corinthians 12:9–10.

  b. What is the last sentence in that passage?

10a. One of my favorite "renamings" in the Bible is one we are never really told about. Mark 2:14 and Luke 5:27 both tell of the same event. What is it?

  b. What is different about this event when we are told about it in Matthew 9:9?

  c. If ever a person was "unaptly" named, it is Levi. The name *Levi* would be a person from the tribe of Levi. The Levites were set aside as ministers of religion, but what is Levi?

d. What do you know about tax collectors? With whom are they generally grouped (Matthew 9:11)?

e. But in the book he penned himself, how does Levi call himself?

I told you earlier what Matthew means. Do you remember? Who better to recognize the gift of God's grace than one called out of a position of hatred to be one of the twelve disciples!

We need to remember that God can rename us, no matter what we have been called until now. Paul says it best in 2 Corinthians 5:17: "Therefore, if anyone is in Christ, he is a new creation. The old has passed away; behold the new has come." Through the water and God's Word at our Baptism, the old has been washed away and we are new in Christ. We have a new name, Christian, and a new identity, beloved. And what God calls us is what we are. He knows us, He loves us, and He calls us by name. We are His!

Prayer of Reflection:

O Father God, despite what others have called me,
despite the names I have sometimes called myself,
thank You that You have given me a new name—
Christian. Help me always to remember that I am
Your beloved child. Help me to reflect that name to
everyone I meet so that they, too, may be made new
in Christ. I pray in His name and for His sake. Amen.

SESSION TWO

CHOSEN

"The LORD your God has chosen you to be a people for His treasured possession, out of all the peoples who are on the face of the earth." Deuteronomy 7:6

Have you ever been on the back side of a two-way mirror? Two-way mirrors are made from coating one side of the glass with a very thin layer of a reflective surface. From one side, a person sees only his or her own reflection, but from the other side of the glass, someone can see into the lighted room as if looking through a window. All the while, the person on the other side is unaware of his presence. Most of the time, they're used by security personnel for anonymous observations and by the police to identify crime suspects.

When I was in college, I worked in campus security. I wore a uniform and had a badge. We had a close working relationship with the local police department. One evening, they asked if we could help with a lineup. I jumped at the chance. I love a good police drama; so what could be more fun than seeing how a lineup really works?

The next afternoon at the prearranged time, two other girls from campus and I went to the police station to participate. First they led us into a room and told us how it would work (it was much like I'd seen on crime shows on television). "Number one, step forward, turn left, turn right, step back." The victim would be on the other side of a two-way mirror, waiting to identify the suspect.

We went into the lineup room and were joined by a fourth girl. Since I knew the other two girls from campus, I assumed this was the alleged perp (do you like my use of crime show lingo?). I glanced at her and thought, "Huh, I look a little like her . . . the same height, same hair color and length; but the other girls look nothing like her—different hair color and length, different body type."

The process began. I was number three. We each stepped forward, left and right and back, just as we were told. Then, after an ominous pause, I heard, "Number three, could you step forward again?" And it suddenly dawned on me. This is not a team I want to be chosen for. No one wants to be picked from a police lineup.

Later I could laugh at being misidentified, but for a brief moment, I thought, "Surely the police know I didn't commit a crime since I volunteered for this, right? Please don't let them pick me."

Although, in that instance, I didn't want to be chosen, there were plenty of other times when I did want to be picked. Raise your hand if you were one of "those people" in elementary

● ● ●

school; one of those who were chosen first for every team, or at least near the first. Strong, fast, coordinated, popular, great at sports. My hand is not up. I wasn't fast. Or strong. Or coordinated. I was usually the "stuck with" one, as in, "Well, I guess we're stuck with Sue." No, they weren't cruel enough to say it out loud, but they didn't have to. I felt it every time I was one of the last two and a team was stuck with me. I'm sure I'm not the only one who knows what it's like to be a "stuck with."

But I do know what it's like to be chosen. My brain is filled with useless information and I'm blessed with the gift of recall, so I'm often chosen first for trivia teams.

It's nice to be among the chosen. Isn't that the way it is? We are chosen (or not chosen) based on our appearance, abilities, talents, and intellect. We're chosen because of what we can bring to the team. We can be thankful that God doesn't choose His team like we choose ours.

1.   According to 1 Samuel 16:7, how does God choose?

In fact, there are two different kinds of looking going on here, according to the Hebrew. As the verse begins, Samuel is told not to consider or look at David's appearance. The Hebrew word here could be translated "to scan." Later in the verse, we are told the Lord looks at or *sees* the heart. It's as if we look at the reflection, but God sees through the mirror to what's on the other side—the inside. When the Lord spoke these words to Samuel, He was referring to the anointing of a king for Israel. We know that David was the choice, despite the fact that he was the youngest of Jesse's sons and not even deemed worthy of a glance by his father (1 Samuel 16:11). We scan the surface; God discerns the heart. And over and over again, God chooses the unlikely.

● ● ●

2. Other than his being the youngest, what do these verses tell us about David?

    a. 1 Samuel 16:12

    b. 1 Samuel 16:18

    c. 1 Samuel 17:50

    d. 1 Samuel 18:14

3a. So, despite the fact that God says He looks not at outward appearances but at the heart, it seems that God made the logical choice, the one any good team captain would make. In fact, what does He call David in Acts 13:22?

But what about us? I'm not a great beauty, a great musician, exceptionally brave, or even always trusting of God. Nor do I do everything God wants me to do. I don't bring much to the team, so why would He choose me? Have you ever wondered this too? One clue comes as we look at God's choice of the nation of Israel.

    b. What does He say in Deuteronomy 7:7–8?

God's choice has nothing to do with us and everything to do with Him. And over and over again, God chooses the unlikely. God chose a murderer (Moses, Exodus 2:11–15) to lead His people out of captivity in Egypt. He chose a child, the eight-year-old Josiah, to be a king (2 Kings 22:1). Eighteen years later, Josiah restored the Book of the Law to its proper place before the people of Israel. God chose a young Jewish girl to win the favor of the king and save her people from their certain destruction "for such a time as this" (Esther 4:14). God chose the shepherds as the first ones to hear the glorious Good News that the Messiah had been born at last (Luke 2:8–18). And God the Son chose lowly fishermen to be the first leaders of His New Testament Church (Peter, James, and John).

4. And then there is Matthew. Read his story in Luke 5:27–32. (He's called Levi here, but we read about his name change in Session 1). What do we find out about Matthew in this passage?

That's right: Matthew is a tax collector. As I write this, April 15 is quickly approaching, and I find that I'm not thrilled with "the tax collector." My kids look at my pay stub. "I don't get it, Mom," one says. "If you make X, why is your paycheck for Y?" Tax collector. Why is the price of gas so high? Tax collector.

Today we don't like them, but in the time of the Bible, tax collectors were not just disliked, they were despised, rejected, and even feared. Many Jews viewed them as traitors because they worked for the hated Roman Empire. Provided they paid to Caesar what was Caesar's, tax collectors were allowed to set their own rates and keep the excess. Notice with whom tax collectors are often grouped (Luke 5:30). And it's to one of these despised that Jesus says, "Follow Me"!

● ● ●

5a. What do we learn about Matthew in Luke 5:28?

Matthew left everything. The Greek word used here means "abandoned." By following Jesus, Matthew turned his back on a lucrative government job. Peter, James, John—all fishermen—walked off the job to follow Jesus but were able to return to fishing to earn their living as they needed to. Matthew, on the other hand, abandoned it all.

    b. What does Matthew do when Jesus calls him, and whom does he invite (Luke 5:29)?

When called to the team, the publican (an official name for tax collector) joins it publicly. Matthew hosts a great feast with a large crowd. I'm thinking he didn't throw the party on a fisherman's budget. And who makes up this large crowd? You guessed it, tax collectors and sinners. (I can hear the Pharisees in my mind as they sneer the word, "sinner," that separates everyone else from themselves.)

    c. Who is it that Jesus chooses for His team, according to Mark 2:17?

How is Matthew integral to the team? He brings his friends and acquaintances to meet Jesus, that they, too, may experience this gift of grace, this gift of God. As a member of God's team, who do you know that you can invite to the party to make His acquaintance and feast with Him?

d. We are not required to change our habits before God will have us on His team. What are we told in Romans 5:8?

I have read that children who are told by their adoptive parents that "we chose you" often wonder what will happen if they mess up—will they be unchosen? What a heavy burden to bear! If I am chosen for my appearance, abilities, or talents, will I be unchosen if those attributes disappear? An athlete with an injury may be dropped from the roster. A pop singer without a second hit becomes a one-hit wonder and fades into oblivion. A beauty queen ages, wrinkles, and becomes a nobody. Unchosen.

Let's look now at one of God's chosen, Aaron. Aaron is not an unlikely choice for God's team. After all, his brother is Moses, and since Moses is "slow of speech and of tongue," he needs someone to speak for him (Exodus 4:10). No, the surprising thing about Aaron is not that he was chosen, but that he didn't get traded when he fell short of the mark.

6. Aaron seems to play the part of Moses' mouthpiece for God well. In addition to speaking on God's behalf for Moses, what does Aaron do in the following verses?

a. Exodus 4:30

b. Exodus 7:10

c. Exodus 7:19–20

Aaron was chosen for the winning team not as a bench warmer but to be a significant part of the action. To speak to world leaders and to God. To perform miracles. When Aaron held up his brother's arm in prayer, the winning team just kept on winning.

In fact, some of us may even envy Aaron's position as a key player on God's team. Have any of you thought, as I have, "If only God would just speak to me, then I would be able to completely follow Him." I don't need a burning bush; a simple email or text message would do.

Aaron received better than that. He was invited to dine with God. Really.

7a. Read Exodus 24:9–11. Who went up to the foot of the mountain with Moses and Aaron? What happened there?

In Exodus 24, Moses, Aaron, Aaron's sons, and the elders see God's feet. Verse 11 tells us that they "beheld" God (NIV "saw"). The Hebrew word *chazah* means "to perceive, to contemplate, to have a vision of." Yes, they perceived God's presence, even if they didn't see His face. And they ate and drank. This was a covenant meal, the sealing of a promise between the people and God, the promise they had made in Exodus 24:3.

b. What was the promise?

It's after this covenant meal that the Lord calls Moses to come up on the mountain to receive the tablets of stone with the laws and commands He had written for their instruction. In Exodus 24:13–14, we see Aaron's true value to the team.

● ● ●

8a. What does Moses tell the elders?

Aaron is left behind as the team captain in Moses' absence. "If anyone has any issues while I'm gone, let him go to Aaron and Hur." Aaron received Moses' complete trust for wise decision-making.

   b. God is also concerned with Aaron's standing before the people. What does Exodus 28:2 say?

   c. Exodus 28:30?

God wants the people to see that Aaron is given dignity and honor and that he has the means to make wise decisions, so He gifts him with sacred garments and a special way to determine the will of God, the Urim and Thummim. When consulted, this visible system from God clearly showed Aaron and the people God's decision.

But the next time we see Aaron, he has fallen flat on his face.

Read Exodus 32:1–6. If you went to Sunday School as a child, I know you know the story. Moses had been on the mountain for forty days (Exodus 24:18). The people behave as though they have given up on seeing him again. I'm intrigued by the way they talk about him in verse 1. The NIV says, "this fellow Moses," as if they have had no relationship with him. And I want Aaron to reply, "He's not just 'this fellow,' he's my brother."

Now Aaron is given his first opportunity to lead the people, not just as Moses had directed but also as the people themselves ask. "Come," they say in the NIV. "Up" in ESV. The root of the word is the Hebrew *alah*, which means "ascend." Today we might see "man up" or "lead us." So Aaron does.

9a. What does Aaron ask for, and what does he do?

My son would describe what happens next as "epic fail." Why a calf? The calf probably resembles Apis, the bull-deity worshiped in Egypt, the most important of all sacred animals there.

b. When they see the calf, what do the people say (v. 4)?

It seems they've totally forgotten Exodus 20:1–3. And Aaron seems to have forgotten the God he heard, saw, and ate a covenant meal with. And I wonder, how is it that Aaron, so soon after experiencing this covenant meal with God, Moses, and the others, would forget who God is, forget the covenant he had made with God, and forget the fellowship meal they had shared?

Then I stop to think about the fellowship meal I share with other believers every week, the covenant meal called Holy Communion, and I recognize that it often doesn't take forty minutes, let alone forty days, to forget God in my life. In fact, some days, it's just the forty seconds from the church door to my car before the grumbling and complaining begin as I respond to my children, who may be sniveling and whining much like those children of Israel.

You too?

10a. When questioned, Aaron adds insult to injury. What is his response to Moses' question (Exodus 32:21–24)? How do you react in the same way (i.e., "They are evil." or "It just happened.")?

• • •

You can see that I just did it above: by blaming my children for my bad mood and my bad decisions, I put myself before the God that I serve. Yes, my fails are just as epic as Aaron's.

    b. What does God say to Moses and, by extension, to Aaron, the children of Israel, and to you and me in Exodus 34:6–7?

    c. After Aaron's epic fail, what does God do, according to Exodus 40:12–13?

I would love this to be the happy ending to Aaron's story—he is forgiven, he is anointed into God's service, and from then on he fails not. That's the way I'd like it to be for me as well: chosen, forgiven, anointed, and from then on sinless. But that isn't my story; nor is it Aaron's. A quick stop at a couple of other locations in the Old Testament will show us more.

    11a. What do Aaron and his sister Miriam do in Numbers 12:1–2? How does God respond in Numbers 12:9–11?

    b. When 250 Israelite men lead a similar rebellion against Moses and Aaron (Numbers 16), God's anger again burns. What does Aaron do (Numbers 16:41–48)?

    c. God tells Moses and Aaron to speak to the rock at Meribah so water would flow from it, yet Moses struck the rock instead. What does God say to Moses and Aaron (Numbers 20:12)?

That's Aaron's pattern. It's our pattern too: trusting in God, failing to trust in God, being forgiven, used by God, trusting in God, failing to trust in God. . . . Yet we are not benched or traded away from the team for our failure. That's because being chosen by God is not about us—it is all about God. His way of choosing is not our way.

    d. What does God say in 1 Corinthians 1:26–30?

Just as God chose David, as He chose Matthew, as He chose Aaron . . . God chooses us to be His children and to bear fruit (John 15:16). Will we fail? Epically. Daily. And daily, through Christ Jesus, we are forgiven and put back into service in God's kingdom. He uses us despite our weaknesses. He uses us *in* our weaknesses. And in our weaknesses, He is strong. What a wonderful God!

Prayer of Reflection

Thank You, God, for choosing me—not because
of what I've done, but because You love me. Help me
to remember that even when I have an epic fail, I am
forgiven and I am loved. And help me to live my life
as one chosen by You, a loving and gracious God.
In Jesus' name. Amen.

SESSION THREE

MORE THAN
MEETS THE EYE

"For I know the plans I have for you, declares the LORD,
plans for welfare and not for evil, to give you a future
and a hope." Jeremiah 29:11

How silly it would be if the dressing room at your favorite
boutique or department store had a pocket mirror on the
wall where the full-length mirror should be. While it might be
good to show you where your makeup needs a touch-up, a
pocket mirror couldn't reveal if the pretty new dress concealed
all your bumps and bulges, if the color of that beautiful sweater
clashed with the new color of your hair, or if that trendy skirt
shows too much leg. A pocket mirror can't let you see the full
picture. And if you can't see the full picture, how will you know
if that new outfit is right for you?

I've been called "crafty" and "creative" by my friends. "You're so artistic," they say. But I can't see it. I do like to scrapbook memories of my children and of vacations. And I sew. That's my grandma's influence coming out. She was a seamstress for real, about a century ago. Today, I'm just a poor imitation, but I can follow a pattern, and often what I sew actually looks like I imagine it will.

One of the things I enjoy about sewing is choosing the fabrics. There are Internet-savvy people out there who shop online for fabrics. Not me. What I see on a website doesn't give me the full picture. A little picture on my computer monitor may show me the details of the pattern, but it won't show me what that fabric looks like from across a room.

Color and pattern are just a small part of the bigger picture. I want to see, touch, and feel. I want to watch how the fabric flows as it moves, to gauge the weight of it as it hangs, to feel the texture with my hands so I can determine whether it is appropriate for the kind of garment I want to make. A silky fabric for a blouse, a crisp gabardine for slacks, cotton for a quilt. I look at it close up and from a distance so I can imagine how it will look when it is finished. More than once I've rejected a pretty fabric because I didn't like the way it felt. It's all about texture. It's *all* about texture.

The children of Israel lived a texture-filled existence. During the time of the prophet Jeremiah, life was bumpy and rough. Kind of burlap-ian; definitely not soft, soothing, and silky. In fact, many of the Israelites had been carried off into exile in Babylon. And to those who had been taken into captivity, God sent a message through the prophet Jeremiah.

Turn to Jeremiah 29:4–6 in your Bible and read a part of that letter now.

1a. What does God tell them to do in captivity?

If you back up to Jeremiah 28, you will see the history that predates this message. Prior to this letter from God through Jeremiah, the captives had been told that within two years, God would break the yoke of captivity (vv. 3–4). The false prophet Hananiah had been persuading the people that very soon they would be returning to their old way of life in Judah; that they may have hit a rough spot, but soon their life would once again be smooth as silk.

    b. What is Jeremiah's response to this prophecy? (Jeremiah 28:6–9)

There's an old saying, "The proof is in the pudding." I'm not sure where that saying comes from, but I do know that this is what Jeremiah is talking about. In essence he says, "I really hope Hananiah is right, and that you all will get to go home soon, but the proof is in the pudding."

    c. When Hananiah persists in his claim that the Israelites will be returning within two years, Jeremiah returns to him with another message (Jeremiah 28:15–16). What is it?

    d. This time, the proof *is* in the pudding. What happens to Hananiah in Jeremiah 28:17?

    e. So, returning to Jeremiah 29, why would God tell the children of Israel to settle in, build houses, plant gardens, get married, and have children?

First of all, by telling them to build, plant, and marry, God is giving them a look at the bigger picture—He is telling them they will be there a while. It's as if He is saying, "Don't be too short-sighted." They'll be there long enough to need something more durable than temporary housing. Long enough to plant and harvest crops. Long enough for their children to get married and for another generation to be born.

Second, I think He is encouraging them to be patient. Don't we tend to become discouraged when things take longer than we want them to? When we don't get an answer as soon as we expect, we think we have been forgotten. God, through Jeremiah, is reminding the people that despite the length of their captivity, He has not forgotten them.

Third, I think God is telling them not to live in the "wouldas and couldas." You know, the looking back, the wishing for everything to be different, the regrets that keep us from moving forward. "Move forward," He says. "Look to the future. Build houses, plant gardens, get married, and have children. See the bigger picture."

    2a. Now, look at Jeremiah 29:7. What else does God tell the people to do?

Three things stand out for me in this verse. **First**, God tells the people to *seek* the welfare (or peace, depending on the translation of the Bible you're reading) of the city where they find themselves. The Hebrew word is *darash*, and it means "to tread or frequent, to follow, to seek, to ask, to care for diligently, to search." Remember, the people have been carried off by an enemy into captivity. They are not where they want to be, and yet they are being told to look for and to help make peace there.

I know when I am in a place in my life where I don't want to be, my tendency is to stomp my feet, kick, and yell (figuratively, usually) to let everyone (my husband, my children) know that I'm not happy. (You know the old saying, "If mama ain't happy, ain't nobody happy.")

The **second** thing that stands out to me in this verse is a phrase that will read differently depending on the translation. Here it is in the King James Version: "whither I have caused you to be carried away captives." You may have to sit on that one for a while. I did. I walked away, prepared dinner, and ate, all while pondering the words that "I"—God—caused you to be carried away, or "carried you into exile" (NIV), or "sent you into exile" (ESV). The Hebrew word is *galah*, and it means "to denude, (by implication) to exile, (captives usually being stripped), bring (carry, lead, go) captive, exile, remove." Does God do that, really? Yes, He does. Really. Does that mean that every time we face a struggle God is bringing us there? Not exactly. It does mean that in every kind of captivity, God either has taken us there or has allowed us to go there. And no, He never abandons us. Perhaps we can be more patient in our struggles if we remember that everything that happens is what God has appointed for us, part of His big-picture plan for us. In the words of Paul: "And we know that for those who love God all things work together for good, for those who are called according to His purpose" (Romans 8:28).

b. **Third**, in Jeremiah 29:7, God says to seek the welfare of the city and pray for it, "for in its welfare you will find your welfare." Jesus says the same thing. Read Matthew 5:43–45 in your Bible and paraphrase Jesus' words here:

_____

_____

_____

_____

_____

An unprecedented concept in the ancient world—working toward and praying for the prosperity of your enemies—this concept still causes wonder today as a mother prays for her child's murderer, a prisoner of war prays for his captors, a single mother prays for the husband who abandoned her and their children when he abandoned his wedding vows.

c. Do you find yourself in a rough, bumpy place—perhaps in exile—at work, at home, or after a falling out with a friend? Maybe your exile comes at the death of a loved one or at the end of an extended illness. If you are in exile, write the cause below.

Have you sought peace in the place where you find yourself? Have you prayed for it? God's promise to the Israelites in captivity was that they could prosper even there.

3a. Notice that while God tells them to marry and have families, He's not telling them to intermarry, to get caught up and intertwined with the Babylonians. He doesn't intend for His people to get established there and stay—it's just a temporary home. What is God's promise in verse 10?

With God, a promise is a promise.

b. What does Joshua tell us in Joshua 23:14?

No, He is not going to leave you in exile; He will bring you back. However, He doesn't promise to do this quickly. Seventy years would have been a lifetime to the Israelites in captivity; our own captivity may seem like a lifetime as well (although we hope not literally seventy years). But again, God's promise is this: I will not abandon you. I will not forget you. And if you have perished before I return, then My promise is for your children. "I will fulfill to you My promise."

    4a. Read Jeremiah 29:11, a verse you are probably familiar with. Write it out here, in whatever translation you are using.

_____

_____

_____

_____

Underline the first two or three words of the verse, depending on your translation. These words are essential to the verse: "I know."

I say, "I wanna know what's going on here," and God says, "I know." I say, "I don't understand what You're doing, God," and God says, "I know." The Hebrew word for "know" is *yada*, and it means "to know, to ascertain by seeing."

    b. What does God tell us in Isaiah 46:10?

    c. And in Revelation 22:13?

God knows the plan because He's the author of the plan; He knows our future because He has seen our future. He is the Alpha and Omega, the Beginning and the End. We say we want to know the future, and God says He wants us to know Him. Read that last sentence again because it is vitally important. We want to know the future, but *God wants us to know Him!*

In the King James Version, the verse begins, "I know the *thoughts* I think toward you." In Hebrew, the word is *machashebeth* and it means "in the concrete, a texture; in the abstract, intention, plan, imagination, purpose, thought." The word for "think" in the KJV is *chasheb*, the root word of *machashebeth*. It means, literally, "to weave or fabricate, to think, regard, or value."

5. Take a minute to look up *texture* in your dictionary. Write a few of its meanings below.

_____

_____

_____

_____

Here are some that I found: "the characteristic structure of the interwoven threads that make up a fabric; an essential or characteristic quality; essence." Often, it's the contrast of textures side by side that create a dramatic element.

Now, what does any of this have to do with Jeremiah 29:11? Try reading the verse this way: "I know the textures I have woven for your life—the smooth places and the rough places." Each makes the other more distinct; the rough places give depth to your character, and the way God has woven your life together is essential to create the character in you that He desires.

Dictionary.com tells me that the word *texture* is from the Latin *texere* (to weave) and is related to the Sanskrit *taksati* (fashions, constructs) and to the Greek word *tekton* (carpenter). Seeing that Greek root, which means "carpenter," I cannot help but think of the son of the carpenter: Jesus. The One who has woven the textures into my life is the One whose essence I am to reflect. The bumpy and the smooth places in my life make the work of Jesus in my life more distinct.

> 6a. Whether they are plans God has for you or thoughts He thinks toward you, what is the next phrase in Jeremiah 29:11?

If you memorized this from the NIV, your answer will read, "plans to *prosper* you and not to harm you." I think that often today's world misunderstands this verse. My dictionary defines *prosper* in the way most of us use the word today: "to be successful or fortunate, especially in financial respects; thrive; flourish." The ESV renders this phrase, "plans for *welfare* and not for evil." My dictionary defines *welfare* as "the good fortune, health, happiness, prosperity, et cetera, of a person, group, or organization." Either way, I think we think "Aha, life is going to be good. God's plans will make me 'healthy, wealthy, and wise.'"

> b. But what are we told in John 16:33?

Is there a contradiction between the Old and New Testaments? Not at all. Perhaps the King James Version will help. The KJV here reads "thoughts of peace, and not of evil." The word for "peace" is *shalom*, a fairly well-known Hebrew word that means "to be safe, well, happy, have health, prosperity, peace." Its root is the Hebrew word *shalam*, which means "to be or to make complete." Evil, on the other hand, has among its Hebrew meanings: "adversity, distress, grief, misery, sorrow, trouble, wretchedness."

God here, then, doesn't promise that the fabric of our lives will be made up of success and fortune; rather, when the warp and woof of the world is adversity, sorrow, trouble, and grief, His plans for us will bring us peace, *shalom*. And it will make us complete.

    c. James tells us a similar thought in his letter. What does he say in James 1:2–4?

    d. What does Paul tell us in Philippians 1:6?

Just as God told the children of Israel in captivity that He wouldn't abandon them, wouldn't leave them (Jeremiah 29:10), He tells us the same. He who began a good work in you will carry it out until completion. He is making you complete. Are you starting to get the full picture?

    7a. Write out the final phrase of Jeremiah 29:11.

_____

_____

_____

_____

_____

    b. What do you think that this means? How do you define "hope"?

Do you define hope the way my daughter does? Every year she hopes to get a horse for Christmas, but because of our family's circumstances, that is not likely to happen. And what about "future"? Is that some time way off in the distance, heaven perhaps? Because if you're like me, that's something that can be easily grasped—that God's plan for me includes eternal life; meanwhile, I'm stuck in the present, and this present stinks. Be honest. Is that what you sometimes think?

In the KJV, these plans for our hope and future read "to give you an expected end." The *expected* part corresponds to *hope* in the other translations and is from the Hebrew *tiqvah*. Literally it means "a cord of attachment." Figuratively it means "expectancy, hope, thing that I long for." The root of this word is *qavah*. This means "to bind together by twisting, to expect, to look patiently, to wait for, on, or upon."

Again I see fibers, the fabric of the fabric: threads. Thread is a tightly twisted strand of two or more plies of fibers, and in the twisting they are made stronger.

    c. What are we told in Ecclesiastes 4:12? Who or what is the third strand?

So, God's plan for you, the texture that He's woven into your life, is interwoven with hope despite the uncertainty and adversity of the warp and the woof of the world. The textures of the trials you face are a lifeline of attachment to the Father, a time when you and God are wrapped together, and you are strengthened by being joined with Him. That's a future and a hope in the midst of the circumstances you face. It's not just the promise of heaven, but a life filled with hope in Christ in the midst of the circumstances you face, knowing that through the adversity you are being made stronger in Christ and more complete in Him.

● ● ●

Even as I write this, I have an image in my mind. It's one you may have seen yourself: a windsock attached to a fixed point on a blustery day. The harder the wind blows, the more the windsock twists, the tighter the cord of attachment becomes, and the closer and closer the windsock gets to the fixed point. It draws up as it is buffeted by the winds and the storm. And so do we. As the storms of life buffet us, we can become more tightly wrapped with Jesus and draw closer and closer to the Father, our fixed point.

8. I don't want to leave out the rest of the passage. As Paul Harvey would say, what's "the rest of the story" in Jeremiah 29:12? What will happen during this time of trial and exile?

Perhaps you, like me, find that you call upon God most when you are experiencing a time of trial, when everything is not all sunshine and roses. That's what the "then" is about in this verse. When then? In seventy years then. When you've experienced hardship and exile then. When life stinks, and the going gets tough, and the children rebel, and the husband loses his job, and the mother gets cancer then.

Are you in a "then" now? If you feel comfortable, share it.

The word translated "come" is *halak*. This same Hebrew word is translated at various places in the Scriptures as run, walk, crawl, float, drive, march, and climb up. And I am reminded that God doesn't care if we walk, run, or crawl. He cares only that we come. And pray. And when we do, He will hear. He *will* listen.

• • •

9a. Finally, write out the words of Jeremiah 29:13 from whatever translation you are using.

_____

_____

_____

_____

_____

When my children were younger, we would sometimes play hide-and-seek, and I'll admit, I sometimes had them hide just to get them out of my hair for a moment or two. When I looked for them, I could find them in an instant—until my daughter reached the age of five or so. Then she became an excellent hider, and I really needed to put in effort to find her. She often didn't respond to "Olly, Olly Oxen Free" (which was our method for crying "Uncle. I give up. Come out, already."), so I had to be vigilant as I looked for her. I had to peek into corners and closets, search behind furniture and under covers.

The word "seek" is the Hebrew *baqash*, and it means "to search out (by any method, specifically by worship and prayer)." God doesn't want a passive-aggressive attitude: "If God wants me, He knows where to find me." He doesn't want a faithless search: "I'll give Him five minutes then I'm trying something else." The Hebrew word tells us exactly how we are to seek God: worship and prayer. We don't have to guess where to look for Him; He doesn't hide. God is present in His Word and in the Sacraments. He is present "where two or three are gathered in [His] name" (Matthew 18:20).

Here's another phrase we should not leave out: "with all your heart."

b. What does God say in Deuteronomy 4:29?

c. How does that play out in 2 Chronicles 15:3–4?

d. I like the words a chapter later in 2 Chronicles 16:9. What does this verse say?

God is constantly on the lookout for people whose hearts are fully committed to Him. He wants you to search Him out wholeheartedly. When we feel like we've been left flapping in the wind, we can be wrapping up in God's encompassing, loving arms. When we seek Him, we see that God is intertwined in our lives, giving us strength and assuring us of hope in Christ.

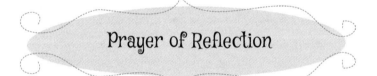

Prayer of Reflection

O God, so often I complain to You about the
adversity of my life. Whether it's for seventy minutes
or seventy days, I don't like it when the days are
bumpy. Help me to know that even when I don't see
the complete picture, Lord, You do. Help me to see
that these are times when I can come closer to You,
times to seek and find You with all of my heart.
In Jesus' name and for His sake. Amen.

SESSION FOUR

BITS AND PIECES
AND A
KALEIDOSCOPE

MIRROR MESSAGE

"As for you, you meant evil against me, but God meant it
for good, to bring it about that many people should be kept
alive, as they are today." Genesis 50:20

Surely you are familiar with the old wives' tale that if you
break a mirror, you'll have seven years of bad luck. Some of
us feel like we've had so much bad luck we must have broken
several mirrors. All the shattered bits and pieces are such a
mess, how can they bring beauty? But pieces of broken glass
are often compiled into beautiful things. Stained glass windows, for example, are made up of smaller pieces of glass, as
are some mosaics and even jewelry.

Broken glass is also used in kaleidoscopes. Have you looked through one lately? You peer through a peephole at one end of the cylinder and see a burst of color and intricate design at the other. Whenever the kaleidoscope moves, even slightly, the design changes and you see the next amazing image. How does a kaleidoscope work? Mirrors. Two mirrors are set at an angle to each other in the cylinder to reflect the bits and pieces of color at the other end—broken glass, buttons, beads, even tiny shells and other bits of nature. The tiny scraps create a beautiful design that lasts only a moment. You never see the same design twice.

Kaleidoscopic designs aren't always limited to the moment, however. Each year since 1974, the city of Houston has played host to the International Quilt Festival. With around 55,000 attendees from all over the globe, this four-day festival is the largest quilt show in the world and the largest convention in the city of Houston. With more than 1,000 booths, 450 classes, lectures, and events, and 2,200 quilts and other textile arts on display, it's quite a scene of kaleidoscopic colors and intricate designs.

One cannot sew and live in Houston for long without hearing about it. And so, curiosity piqued, I went, dragging my husband along for the trip downtown. We were both amazed. My husband, who went only because he loves me, was intrigued by the hundreds of designs. These were not my grandmother's quilts, they were works of art: beautiful and stunning collections of colors, patterns, and hues, masterfully stitched. Many times you would find a woman wearing white gloves standing next to a quilt, ready to show the back if you were interested. No greasy, sweaty, Dorito-orange fingers were allowed to mar these spectacular quilts.

The first step in quilt-making is choosing the pattern. The next step requires a trip to a fabric store to buy quarter- and

● ● ●

half-yard lengths of fabric in contrasting lights and darks to create the pattern. The fabric then gets cut into precise triangles, rectangles, or squares. (Funny, a quilter takes perfectly good fabric, cuts it up into tiny pieces, and then puts it back together.) Precision matters. Being even one-sixteenth of an inch off in cutting or sewing can drastically alter the finished product.

What makes a quilt interesting to me is the hundreds, perhaps thousands, of fabric pieces sewn together, contrasting between lights and darks to create visual texture. And with the visual texture comes the beauty. Without a master plan and a master's hand, a quilt is just scraps of fabric joined at the seams. But with a plan and a master's hand, it is art. Truly, little scraps of nothing become a masterpiece.

In the last lesson, we saw that God's plan for our lives includes the texture that makes His presence in our lives more apparent. Remember, in that lesson we established that based on the definitions of the Hebrew words used, Jeremiah 29:11 could read, "I know the textures I have woven for your life." Texture, whether tactile (rough and smooth) or visual (light and dark), is essential for depth of character. God uses texture in our lives to bring us to completion and draw us closer to Him. He has a plan not just for the rough and the smooth places, but for the scraps in our lives as well.

Jacob's son Joseph lived a highly textured life, and his story begins with the gift of a textile, a richly ornamented robe: wearable art, a coat of many colors. Let's take a quick look at the tapestry of Joseph's life to see how richly textured it was, with times of silky-smoothness and times of rough, knotty texture; and with times of light and dark. His story begins in Genesis 37.

1. Which visual textures of light and dark stand side by side in Genesis 37:3–4?

Love, hate, and sibling rivalry . . . something that never happens around my house. Yeah, right. I'm guessing that if you have children or siblings, you've experienced it to some extent yourself. "You love her more than me." "That's not fair. You never make him do it." Whether real or imagined, such conflict is just one of the ways the fabric of our lives is scrapped and shredded. It may be minor and almost insignificant in your home, or, like at Jacob's house, it may be destructive.

2a. Skim Genesis 37:5–11 to see how the situation at Jacob's house grew worse. What happened, and how does Jacob finally respond?

I was intrigued to see that what Joseph interprets in his dreams is exactly the blessing Jacob's own father, Isaac, had pronounced over Jacob when he experienced his own case of sibling rivalry, which culminated in him stealing his brother Esau's birthright (Genesis 27:27–29). It seems that fabric had been building up in this family scrap bag for years.

b. How did Esau react to his brother's deception? (Genesis 27:41)

And so Jacob fled, and the life of Isaac's family was tattered and torn.

But let's return to Jacob's son. As Joseph's dreams of future grandeur are interwoven with the jealousy and hatred of his brothers, the unthinkable happens. Read Genesis 37:18–28.

● ● ●

3a. What do his brothers plot, and what do they do?

   b. How do the brothers cover up the deception?
      (Genesis 37:31–34)

The texture in Joseph's life continues to alternate between rough and smooth, light and dark, as his story proceeds in Genesis 39 and Joseph prospers as a servant in Potiphar's household. Notice the transitions between his life's textures as you skim Genesis 39.

   c. How do real pieces of fabric also play a key role in this part of Joseph's life story?

4a. Now, pause briefly at verse 21. What are we told?

Despite being enslaved, despite being imprisoned, God shows Joseph love and gives him *favor*. Grace. The Hebrew word is *chen*, and its root is the word *chanan*, which means "to bend or stoop in kindness to an inferior." *Chanan* is when a king bends down to a commoner, when a lord bows down to a servant, when the God of the universe humbles Himself to become a baby in a manger and then grows to be a man who dies on the cross for the sins of the world. Joseph felt *chanan*, even in this rough, dark place in his life. You and I can feel it too.

● ● ●

b. I can imagine Joseph using the words of Paul in
1 Timothy 1:12–14. Summarize what Paul says here:

_____

_____

_____

_____

And I imagine Joseph experiences *shalom*, peace, as God's goodness overlays the fabric of adversity in Joseph's life.

Joseph's story continues as he interprets dreams, finds favor with the pharaoh, and eventually rises to the highest favor possible in the land (Genesis 41:39–41). Joseph is eventually used by God not only to save the people of Egypt (where he was once enslaved and imprisoned), but also to save the very lives of his brothers who had thrown him into the pit in the first place. If you don't know the story, take time to read Genesis 37–50. You won't be sorry you did. Otherwise, for now, focus on the end of the story, Genesis 50:20. Write out the first half of the verse here:

_____

_____

_____

_____

Guess what? Here we find the Hebrew word *chasheb* again, from our last lesson—to weave. The KJV reads, "But as for you, ye *thought* evil against me; but God *meant* it unto good, to bring to pass, as it is this day, to save much people alive." Joseph is saying to his brothers, "The cloth of sorrow, misery, and trouble you meant to weave was instead a cloth that God wove

● ● ●

for good, for the saving of many lives." In Joseph's life, we see that the threads of favoritism, pride, sibling rivalry, jealousy, betrayal, false accusation, and false witness all are woven into a tapestry of love and grace and to the saving of many lives. And in fact, your life and mine are included in this salvation act because the family of Joseph and his brothers become the twelve tribes of Israel, the children of God, to which you and I are spiritual heirs according to Galatians 3:29.

5. Can you see how God has pieced together scraps in your life for His purposes? Share them here, and if you are comfortable, share them with your group.

The fabric of Lazarus's life is not smooth, either. When we first hear of him in John 11:1, he is ill, and before we have a chance to meet him, he has died. In fact, in our first view of Lazarus (John 11:44), he is wrapped in linens, "binding cloths" the Greek tells us; he is wearing the clothes of his burial four days prior. Read Lazarus's story now, John 11:1–46.

6a. Certainly death is not what his sisters had expected when they sent word to Jesus. What was that message (John 11:3)?

Notice what they call Lazarus: "he whom You love." Certainly they had reason to expect that Jesus would come immediately to help their brother. He has healed total strangers, cast out demons from wild men, and taken time to heal the servant of a centurion (a hated Roman soldier, read that "enemy"). Would He not come quickly to help "he whom [He loved]"? No. Jesus' response is not to hurry, but to tarry.

b. What does He do (v. 6)?

This is hard for us to fathom if we believe that the cloth God creates for us will make life easy, wrinkle-free, effortless. And good Christians that we are, we hate to admit that this is something we want to believe. We've given our lives to Jesus. We call Him "friend." Now life should be easy, prosperous.

7.   Both of Lazarus's sisters (Martha and Mary) greet Jesus in a similar fashion. What do they say (vv. 21, 32)?

I cannot speak for you, but I can speak for myself. The words that Martha spoke, the words that Mary spoke, the words of friends standing nearby (v. 37) are words that I would never say. Aloud. But I have thought them. "Surely God, if You had been here. . . ." The unspoken thought behind the spoken word? "God, You have made a mistake." Do you dare admit that you've had the thought before? That you had dared to think that perhaps God was sleeping on the job? That He wasn't pulling His weight? That He wasn't where He was supposed to be when He was supposed to be there? "If You had been here, my brother would not have died." Words from a broken heart, when the fabric of life has been torn in two. Write any thoughts you have here:

So, why do bad things happen to good people? Why, when we need Him most, does God sometimes seem so distant? Why, if His plan is to prosper us and not to harm us, does He allow the hurt, death, illness, unemployment, and estrangement? I can give you the Sunday School answer, "sin in the world" (which is true), but I can also give you the words of Jesus.

8a. Read John 11:4. Write the words here:

_____

_____

_____

_____

_____

This "illness" ("sickness" in the NIV) is the Greek word *astheneia*, which means "feebleness or frailty." Astheneia comes from a root word that means "strengthless." So let's agree that it could refer not only to sickness, but also to any areas where we are "strengthless," such as those I just mentioned.

b. Is there an area of your life right now in which you are "strengthless"?

The next phrase is "does not lead to death" (ESV) or "will not end in death" (NIV). And yet it does. In John 11:14, we are told that Lazarus has died. So what does Jesus mean "this sickness will not end in death" (NIV)? First, that's not where the story ends, as we see in a few more verses. But second, the phrase is not about death, it's about something else, something more. "It is for the *glory* of God, so that the Son of God may be *glorified* through it." *Glory* is *doxa*. It means "dignity, glory, honor, praise, worship." When it is used the second time ("glorified"), it is *doxazo*, and it has the additional meaning "to magnify." The root of the word means "to be apparent." My husband likes to remind me that when we use a magnifying glass, it doesn't change the character of the thing we are looking at. It just magnifies what we see. It makes it bigger, more obvious, more clear. And so, when Jesus says it is so that the Son of God may be glorified, or magnified, He is saying that this is happening so that we may clearly see God, His presence, His character.

I want to pause on this word for a minute and look at some other places in the New Testament where the same Greek word is used. What brings glory to God, what magnifies Him and helps us to see Him more clearly, in each of the following verses?

9a. Matthew 15:31

b. Luke 17:15

c. Mark 2:10–12 (careful, this might be a trick question)

Lazarus would die, but in his death, because of his death, through his death, God would be worshiped, honored, and glorified. He would be magnified and He would be very apparent. In fact, this is the situation with Lazarus not simply because he dies, but because Jesus raises him from the dead. We see it in John 11:45.

● ● ●

d. What happens?

e. But we also see it before Lazarus is raised in an exchange between Martha and Jesus. Read the exchange, John 11:21–27. How is God glorified, magnified, and made apparent here?

Martha professes that Jesus is the Christ, the Messiah, the Son of God, and God is glorified. Furthermore, Jesus reveals Himself as the resurrection and the life, and that belief in Him will bring eternal life. Martha believes, and God is glorified.

What about you and the situation you face? Might it be to bring God glory? To magnify Him in and through your life? God's desire is not simply to carry you through a trial that you might be facing, but to reveal Himself to you through the trial, as He revealed Himself to Martha.

Let's take a look at a few more places where *doxazo* is used:

- Matthew 5:16

- 1 Peter 4:11

- John 12:16–17

We are to be lights to the world, lights that magnify God's power and His grace. Through our words and actions, through our service, when God acts miraculously in our lives—and even if He doesn't provide the miracle we think He should—God calls us to magnify Him.

When Addi was diagnosed with brain cancer when she was just eighteen months old, hundreds of people in her family, church family, and social media contacts set about in prayer, fully believing that God could and would heal her. Through thirteen surgeries, heavy doses of chemotherapy, and powerful radiation treatments, they persevered in prayer. And yet God chose to bring this sweet girl to her heavenly home just days before her second birthday. This story could have ended with "God, if You had been there, my little girl would not have died." Instead, Addi's parents have used every opportunity to bring glory and honor to Jesus, praising God for all the ways He was with them throughout the storm of cancer. And they have continued to magnify God through their lives as they have set up Addi's Faith Foundation (www.AddisFaithFoundation.org) to support research for finding a cure for childhood cancer, as well as to support other families who find themselves living in the same storm. To date, they have raised more than $450,000. When I asked Addi's mom, Amber, if I could tell a little piece of her story, she responded, "Yes, and to God be the glory."

Surely God might bring you a miracle as He brought one for Mary, Martha, and Lazarus. But it could be that He won't. Will you rely on Jesus words, "This illness (trial, time of suffering) does not lead to death"? Will you trust in His words and rely on His grace to carry you through the trial to a place where God is glorified through it? Perhaps it will bring an affirmation of your faith, an outward display or an inward trust in God's power in your life whatever the outcome. Can you believe the words of Jesus, "This _____is for the glory of God, so that the Son of God may be glorified through it"?

Maybe it will weave a cord of attachment, and as you rely on His grace and mercy to carry you through the trial, it will bind you closer to Him, as God pieces together a beautiful tapestry of His love for you. God can and will take the scraps of your life, and when they are placed in His hands, He will create a glorious work. You are His masterpiece, and your life is a light to His presence.

In closing this lesson, do you want to know something else about a kaleidoscope? Besides mirrors (or other reflective surfaces) and bits and pieces to reflect, there's one other thing needed to make a kaleidoscope work: a light source. There must be light to illuminate the objects. Hmmm. When God brings His light to the bits and scraps and broken places of your life, surely He can make those places beautiful.

Prayer of Reflection

Father God, You not only created me but also

redeemed the scraps of my life, fabricating them into

a work of art that magnifies You. Help me to see those

places in my life where it seems You've come too late

as places meant to magnify Your presence in my life.

And help me to magnify You in all that I do. In Jesus'

name and for His sake. Amen.

SESSION FIVE

A SERVANT'S
HEART

"For we are His workmanship, created in Christ Jesus for
good works, which God prepared beforehand, that we
should walk in them." Ephesians 2:10

A couple of lessons ago, we talked about how unproductive it
would be to use a pocket mirror in a dressing room. It's the
wrong mirror for the job. Likewise, you don't need a full-length
mirror when you tweeze your eyebrows, but a lighted makeup mirror would serve you well. And really, your car's rearview
mirror is not the best place to apply lipstick (especially when
you are driving!). Each different kind of mirror serves a specific
purpose. And while any mirror can be used in more than one
way, most are designed to work best in specific circumstances.

For instance, many of us have a full-length mirror to check our appearance from head to toe before we leave home. When your reflection shows all of you at one time, you can see if you need to make adjustments. You can step closer to the mirror to inspect your makeup as you would with a pocket mirror, or you can step back and turn to the side to get a different perspective. Do you need to wear a slip, for instance, or are your shoes appropriate?

One year, the day before Easter, my daughter wanted a girl's day out. She had just celebrated her tenth birthday and had a gift card that was burning a hole in her pocket. She needed new shoes to wear with her Easter dress. And she had a third request. "Mom, can we get our nails done?"

Brianna loves to get her nails done. She has more colors of nail polish than anyone I know, and she has been polishing her nails since she was two (after Aunt Carolyn polished nails at Christmas, Brianna came home and polished hers with yogurt). By age four, Brianna was giving manicures to everyone in the family at Christmas (including her teenage cousin Luke.) And by the time she was eight, she had amassed her collection of polish. For my part, I am not so into nail polish. Aside from a brief period in the early '90s when I had acrylic nails for about six months, I've had my nails done professionally exactly twice—on my wedding day eighteen years ago and on my sister's wedding day three years before. Brianna often begs to polish my nails, but I usually dissuade her or get her to agree to polish just my toes with a nice bright pink to show when I wear sandals.

But on that day before Easter, she begged, "Please, Mom!" and I agreed to the manicure. Brianna decided on French manicures for both of us, and about half way through the manicure, I realized we had a problem. Both Brianna and I were wearing new sandals with our Easter dresses the next day and still needed our toenails polished so our Easter best would be complete from head to toe. The problem was that I didn't want to pay for

● ● ●

pedicures too, but we had polish on our toenails that would have to come off. If we removed it ourselves, it would ruin our beautiful manicures. What to do?

The only solution was waiting at home. And that's how the night before Easter, my husband—the worship leader—sat on the floor with cotton ball in hand and removed the polish from our toes. "If Jesus could wash the disciples' feet, I suppose I could get nail polish off your toes," he said kindly. He has a servant's heart.

1a. God has created us to be His servants. In fact, Paul spells it out in Ephesians 2:10. Write out the words here:

_____

_____

_____

_____

The Greek for *workmanship* has the connotation of a work of art. You are God's masterpiece, His work of art. Yet you're not just a work of art to be placed on the wall and admired. You are a work created with a purpose in mind. God has had a plan for your life from the very beginning.

As a mother with young children and a VCR, I watched plenty of Disney movies, over and over and over again. One of our favorites was *Beauty and the Beast*, which we watched more than a time or two. I love it when Belle meets the staff at Beast's castle, the staff that had been enchanted into very animated inanimate objects. Mrs. Potts, the housekeeper, can't help but welcome the newcomer and make her feel at home despite the fact that she has been turned into a teapot. Similarly, Lumière, the butler, continues to buttle, even though he's been turned into a candelabra. They are servants created to serve. It's what they were made for, and it would be unsettling for them not to do what they were created for.

   b. Perhaps I'm drawn to them because that is our calling in Christ Jesus. Jesus spells it out in Matthew 20:26. According to this verse, how does anyone become great?

While the world is teaching that the great are the powerful, the wealthy, those who are served, Jesus tells us that whoever wants to be first must be a slave. Hmmm.

   2. What happens when a servant is not serving? Let's take a look at David's life. Read 2 Samuel 11:1–5. When do the events of this story take place?

Did you catch it? It was the season for battle, when kings lead their men, but David didn't "went," he "sent." And he hung out in the safety of Jerusalem, but he knew the job he should be doing. He knew the place he should be—at battle with his men, destroying the Ammonites.

How unsettling to be a servant who isn't serving. David can't sleep. So he *walks* on his rooftop. The Hebrew word used here has various meanings, including "to pace, to exercise, to wander, to march," and the one that strikes me now: "to be wont to haunt." Is David pacing, perhaps, haunted by the knowledge that he should be serving with his men? It's unnerving for a servant not to be serving. And David's eye catches a vision of Bathsheba, a beautiful woman bathing on another nearby roof-

● ● ●

top. You know the story—he inquires after her, she comes, and God's commands are broken. She conceives a child, which sets off plans of deception and finally murder.

I'm struck by the fact that David was walking on the rooftop for another reason. Remember the verse you read a few minutes ago from Ephesians 2:10? "We are His workmanship, created in Christ Jesus for good works, which God prepared beforehand, that we should *walk* in them." Instead of walking in the good works that God had prepared for him, the service God had planned for him, David walked on a rooftop, avoiding the very service he had been called to do.

    b. When we aren't serving as God calls us, what kind of rooftop walking are we doing? Shopping? Surfing the Web? Eating? Watching an inappropriate amount of television? Spending hours on the phone or on Facebook? What about you—what kind of rooftop walking can you get caught up in?

We can get into trouble just like David when we walk away from the service to which God is calling us, the service He has prepared for us.

Then there's our friend Moses. Thirty-nine times in the Bible we find God saying "my servant Moses" or hear the phrase "Moses, the servant of God." But let's look at how Moses' service to God began. As God comes to Moses in the burning bush, He calls him into service. Read Exodus 3:9–15 and 4:1–10.

Oh, how I can relate to Moses. I have been very good at telling God why I cannot possibly serve in the way He has asked. Here's an example: Years ago, I was attending a Bible study on Tuesday mornings at church with about eight to ten other women. When the leader of the group said she was moving because her husband was being transferred, several of the women said, "Susan, you should lead." I think they thought since I had been a teacher in my previous life (before moving to Texas), I was the logical replacement. But I taught English, not religion; teenagers, not women. I was uncomfortable on parent night, talking to adults. And way back when I taught junior high in a Lutheran school and my principal told me I'd need to teach religion, I said, "I think the pastor should teach it."

So, when these women asked me to lead Bible study, I told them no, and I told God, "Who am I to do this?" and "What will I say?"

I gave God other excuses as well: "I have a job, and sometimes I have to work on Tuesday mornings." So God gave me a promotion, and put me in charge of scheduling. "I'm not very good at organizing details," I said, so God gave me Cricket, a behind-the-scenes, quiet woman in the Bible study, who said, "Susan, if you teach the class, I'll take care of all the other details, like refreshments, room reservations, and childcare." I remember thinking, "**What if no one comes?**" very similar to Moses' "What if they do not believe me or listen to me?" (Exodus 4:1, NIV). Well, the first day of the new semester eighteen women came to sit around a conference table built for ten. God is so good!

3a. I remember very clearly that first day of class thinking, "**I don't know what to talk about, and I don't know how to pray out loud.**" Then I remembered the words God spoke to Moses in Exodus 4:12. Write those words here:

_____

_____

_____

_____

_____

● ● ●

The word *go* is interesting. The Hebrew word is *yalak*. Among its definitions are "walk (remember that Ephesians verse), march, pursue, grow, lead," and a curious one, "be weak." Paul talks about serving in weakness in 2 Corinthians 12:9, as he discusses his "thorn in the flesh."

b. Although three times he begged God to remove the weakness, what did the Lord say instead?

When I go in *my* weakness, God fills me with His strength. In fact, I could rewrite the verse and say, "Now be weak, and I will help you speak."

c. Head back to Exodus 4 for a minute. We skipped verse 11. After Moses gives one more excuse—"I'm not a good speaker"—how does God respond?

God asks Moses, and He asks me as well: "Who made you?" It's a rhetorical question, but it's one worth thinking about. The word *gave*, or *made* (depending on the translation), can be translated "appointed, charged, considered, ordained, placed, preserved, purposed, regarded." And God answers, "Is it not I, the Lord?" He tells Moses, "I made you and every aspect of you. I've considered your mouth and your speaking ability. I've regarded you, placed you, ordained you, and charged you. I've purposed you, and your mouth, to carry My message."

• • •

d. He says the same to us. What is it that God has called you to do, and what excuses have you tried to put in His way? **I'm not a good speaker, a good pray-er, a good hostess? I don't know what to say? I'll mess up? I don't have the intellect, the time, the skill, the money?** Reflect on any excuses you may have used recently to not serve God as He has called you to. God knows you intimately, and He created you perfectly for His purpose.

I rejoice in the fact that God repeatedly calls Moses, "My servant" not "My reluctant servant," because in the end, despite the excuses, Moses went and was used mightily by God to lead his people out of slavery.

Please don't misunderstand me. God isn't calling you every single time someone asks you to serve on a committee, to teach Sunday School, or (you fill in the blank). Such service may be for a great cause, but that doesn't mean that *God* is calling you to do it.

4a. I know you know the story of Mary and Martha—we're women, and we know this one. Read it again now in Luke 10:38–42. What do you learn about Martha? What do you think this looked like?

"Distracted," my Bible says. She was doing, doing, doing. The KJV renders it like this: She "was cumbered about much serving." She was serving the Lord, cleaning, cooking, and so forth. There's always so much that can be done when we're serving the Lord. The tasks never end. And serving isn't bad;

● ● ●

it's what we were put here to do. Remember Ephesians 2:10:
"We are [God's] workmanship, created in Christ Jesus for good
works." We were created to take action, to serve. But Martha's
actions on behalf of Christ had become distractions. I imagine
that her list of worthy activities, her "to-do list," was a mile long.

    b. How does Jesus answer her complaint about her sister's
       laziness ("Lord, do You not care that my sister has left
       me to serve alone?" [Luke 10:40])?

    The Greek used in Jesus' response in verse 41 could be
rendered so: "You are distracted and crowded by the plenteous."
He isn't scolding her for the activities she's doing but rather
reminding her that one thing is most important—that she not
neglect the time to sit at Jesus' feet to hear Him speak.

    Not every phone call for help is a call from God. I think
sometimes the enemy tries to distract us with many worthy
activities. The word *distract* in the Greek is translated "to drag all
around." This is not the activity that God has ordained for us.
Jesus' promise is that He has come that we may have abundant
life (John 10:10), life that fills us up, not drags us down.

    5a. What is Moses' prayer in Psalm 90:17?

    The word translated "favor" in the NIV and ESV is *no 'am*
in Hebrew. Among its meanings are "beauty, delight, grace,"
and the one that most fits our application here, "suitableness."
When we pray that God *establishes* the work of our hands, the
Hebrew is *kuwn*. This Hebrew word is full of meanings, among
them, "to prepare, be fitted, confirm, direct."

b. Use these words to write Moses' prayer in your own words.

As I pray these words in trying to decide what tasks God has called me to, I can pray, "God, prepare me for the work that You have established; direct and confirm me in the task that is suitable for me."

So what work has God established for you? God has deliberately shaped you to serve Him in a unique way. Look again at Ephesians 2:10. "For we are [God's] workmanship, created in Christ Jesus for good works, which God _____." The Greek word translates "fit in advance." We are fit, shaped, for a purpose. Rather than try to fit a square peg in a round hole, we need to find out what works God has established for us. In fact, God has designed the exact place for our PEG to fit, based on our **P**assion, **E**xperiences, and **G**iftedness.

Passion describes the bundle of desires, hopes, interests, dreams, ambitions, and affections you have. It is the source of all your motivations—what you love to do and what you care about the most. What does your heart beat for? That's your passion. God wants to use your passion for His service. After all, He's the one who created that passion in you.

6. Mark 12:30 spells it out. How are we to love God?

God allows your **Experiences** in life for the purpose of molding you, to equip you for ministry. Life experiences happen with family, friends, and even strangers in educational, vocational, spiritual, and ministry settings; they can be happy or even painful. God never wastes a hurt! For God to use your painful experiences, you must be willing to share them. The wounds you've resented or regretted most in life, the ones you've wanted to hide and forget, can be used to help others.

7. Think about Moses for a minute. Placed in the Nile in a basket as a baby, he was raised in the pharaoh's home. What better experience could he have had to make him a leader? What experiences have you had (yes, even painful ones) that God can use in His service?

Write out the words of 2 Corinthians 1:4 as a reminder of what God would have us do with our painful experiences.

_____

_____

_____

_____

_____

Your **Giftedness** is the natural talents you were born with. Some people have a natural ability with words. Some are athletic. Some are artistic, musical, or mechanical. Some have the ability to grow plants; others have the ability to grow money. All our abilities are gifts from God. God will never ask you to dedicate your life to a task you have no talent for. On the other hand, the abilities you do have are a strong indication of where God wants you to serve. They are clues to knowing God's will for you.

8a. Do you have a special talent or ability that you believe God wants you to use in His service?

Don't think that you do? Take a look at the story of Ehud, in Judges 3:12–23. (It's a little gory; sorry.) As you read, see if you can figure out what makes Ehud special.

Did you catch it? Ehud's special gift was left-handedness. Some of you may have this gift and find it more of an annoyance, especially when you try to use scissors. But in Ehud's case, he was able to sneak in an eighteen-inch sword strapped to his right thigh, for use with his left hand, and he was able to defeat the evil king Eglon of the Moabites.

    b. In Joppa, there was a woman named Tabitha, sometimes called Dorcas. What special talent or ability did she use in God's service (Acts 9:36–39)?

    c. She was so well-loved that she was given another special gift . . . new life (Acts 9:40–42). You have been given new life in Christ as well. So, what special gifts—athletic, artistic, mechanical, financial, and so on—has God given you for use in His service?

I have a friend with a compassion for people and a *passion* for writing. She *experienced* the sudden death of her husband. She has a *gift* for organization (as a mother of six children, she'd have to). She now writes a blog and serves as a fund-raiser for a national organization designed to support young widows. Although it's not the life she envisioned when she was younger, it is the hole God designed for her PEG.

    9a. Take a few minutes to examine your PEG. Where has God designed you for service?

Passions:

Experiences:

Giftedness:

b. Now that you have learned about your PEG, is there
   currently an area where you are serving that is a square
   to your round? On the other hand, is there an area of
   service in your community, school, church, or place
   of employment that you hesitated to become involved
   in but that you now see fits your shape?

c. Looking at your PEG can help you see how you are
   created in Christ Jesus to do the works God prepared in
   advance for you to do. According to 1 Peter 4:10, how
   should we serve one another?

Real service starts in the mind. Attitude is everything.
Listen to how God describes Caleb in Numbers 14:24 in the NIV:
"My servant Caleb has a different spirit and follows me wholeheartedly." That's how I want to be described as well. It's what
we are called to do in Ephesians 6:7 (NIV): "Serve wholeheartedly-
ly, as if you were serving the Lord, not people."

As followers of Christ, we are being called not just to attend
a worship service every Sunday, but to recognize that our service
is a form of worship.

10a. How is this spelled out in Ephesians 5:1–2?

I love that the ESV begins verse 2 with these words, "And *walk* in love. . . ." It so easily ties this verse in with the beginning of our lesson.

We serve God, we worship God, when we serve others. There is no separating the worship from the service when we do it wholeheartedly, as if serving God, not man. Our worship doesn't spring from compulsory service either.

    b. What does 2 Corinthians 9:7 tell us about our gift of service?

The same truth for how we give our offerings to God can apply to how we offer our service to God. Read on in the chapter and you'll see, "for the ministry of this service is not only supplying the needs of the saints but is also overflowing in many thanksgivings to God" (v. 12). Our service as an act of worship leads others to worship the God we serve.

Our worship and our service are a response to all that God has done for us.

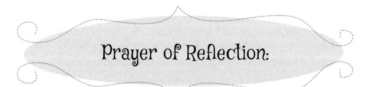

Prayer of Reflection:

Thank You, God, that when You created me You had
purpose in mind. When I reflect on my life, help me
to see what You see, what purpose I am designed for,
and then help me to act in service of love. In Jesus'
name. Amen.

SESSION SIX

ROYALTY

MIRROR MESSAGE

"See what kind of love the Father has given to us, that we should be called children of God; and so we are." 1 John 3:1a

I love to travel . . . plane, train, or automobile, it matters not how. I just love to see the world, and I've been so blessed to be able to do so. I've been blessed to travel to all fifty states and to Mexico, Europe, and Africa. My trip to Europe stands out in my mind now. I went with a friend after my second year of teaching. With everything we needed in backpacks, my friend and I set off for five weeks in Europe. No schedule, no reservations; just traveling wherever we felt like, on whatever train we happened to catch.

We saw plenty of castles and palaces, all homes of the rich and famous and powerful rulers of medieval Europe, including Neuschwanstein Schloss in the Bavarian Alps, the inspiration for Disney's Cinderella's castle, and the 350-room home of Louis XIV, the Palace of Versailles, resplendent in its garish wealth. One of the most famous rooms in the palace is the Hall of Mirrors. Constructed under Louis XIV's guidance, every aspect of its construction glorified him. The hall features 17 large windows opposite 17 mirrored arches, with each arch composed of 21 mirrors for a total of 357 mirrors! These mirrors reflect the sunlight from the windows onto the tableaux painted on the ceiling—thirty images representing and glorifying the narrative of his life that the king wanted others to know. In the time of Louis XIV, the impressive and imposing hall was bound to make visitors feel small and insignificant as they waited to see the king.

But perhaps my most memorable moment occurred on our first full day in England, when we ventured out to Buckingham Palace to see the Changing of the Guard. When the hostess of the B&B where we were staying asked what our plans were for the day, we told her we were heading into London. We should have suspected something was up by the way she raised her eyebrow and said, "You're crazy to go today. I suspect it may be a bit crowded," in that very understated British way. ("Really," we thought, "so are New York City and Chicago on a beautiful summer day. What's the big deal?") And we were off.

As we emerged from the Underground, we met throngs of people. Now, I know the Changing of the Guard is a popular tourist attraction, and since it occurs only once a day crowds often gather, but I was surprised to see thousands of people lining the streets. So we pushed, prodded, and elbowed our way through the crowd to get a look.

● ● ●

At least a hundred of the Royal Guard lined the street. Before long a marching band came down the street, then several units on horseback. We learned that this was not the Changing of the Guard. In fact, it was the queen's birthday, which is celebrated with "The Trouping of the Colour," a parade of royal magnitude.

Marching bands and horsemen were just the beginning of the ceremony that included royalty—Queen Elizabeth II, Prince Philip, Princess Diana, Prince Charles, the Queen Mum, and Prince Andrew all were present, with the queen on horseback, the Princess in a Cinderella-style carriage, and more than a few Rolls Royces. All this was barely fifty feet away; royalty, *waving right at me!* This processional to celebrate her highness was amazing!

That royal parade reminds me of another and of a wee little man named Zacchaeus. Read his story in Luke 19:1–10.

1. When I read his story, I find myself wondering, did Zacchaeus set out to see Jesus that day, or was it just a happy accident like mine? Either way, since he is "small of stature" and unable to elbow his way to the front, what does Zacchaeus do to see Jesus?

I like the word used for "small of stature," *mikroterus*. In addition to small in size, quantity, or number, it also means small in dignity, and I can't imagine a grown man doing anything less dignified than hiking up his robe and shimmying up a sycamore tree to get a look at what's happening right in front of him.

2a. While I only imagined the British family waving right at me, Zacchaeus's encounter with the King was much different. What does Jesus do in Luke 19:5?

I like the way it is rendered in the KJV: "And when Jesus came to the place, He looked up and saw him, and said unto him, 'Zacchaeus, make haste, and come down; for to day I must abide at thy house.'"

Now, do this former English teacher a favor and underline the verbs in that verse. Did you underline "came," "looked," "saw," and "said"? Great! What the KJV does that the ESV doesn't is separate the words *looked* and *saw*. The first word is *anablepo*, and it means simply "to look up." But the second word is *eido*, which means "to see, to know, to perceive, to understand."

> b. Jesus didn't simply see an undignified man in a tree, He saw a man and understood his desperate need for a king, *the* King, Jesus. And He wastes no time in entering Zacchaeus's life. What does Jesus say?

When Jesus says, "I must stay at your house today," He is saying that it's imperative that He stays with Zacchaeus. It's not necessary for Jesus, as in there's no other place to stay, there's no room at the inn; but it is necessary for Zacchaeus to open his heart and his home to Jesus. Jesus sees and understands Zacchaeus's needs, even if Zacchaeus doesn't fully recognize them himself. It was curiosity that drove Zacchaeus to the indignity of climbing the tree that day, but that is right where he met his Savior and King.

> 3a. How did Zacchaeus respond? (Luke 19:6)

The same Greek word (*chairo*) is used just a few verses later (Luke 19:37) as crowds gather on what we know as Palm Sunday to rejoice and welcome their King, who is riding on the back of a donkey.

● ● ●

b. Back to Zacchaeus—what was his response to this visit from Jesus, from welcoming Jesus into his home? (Luke 19:8)

c. And how does Jesus reply? (Luke 19:9–10)

Zacchaeus was a wealthy man, the chief tax collector we are told, and as such he had much to offer his Lord and King. Perhaps it would appear to some that he bought his salvation, but Jesus recognizes him not as a wealthy man, but as one who is lost.

Sometimes we have nothing to offer a king. In fact, we *never* have anything to offer the King, the Lord of the universe, who created all things and in whom all things live and move and have their being (Acts 17:28). When we think that we are saved because of some goodness on our part, we fail to recognize our own helplessness.

4a. One man who totally recognized his own helplessness, however, was Mephibosheth. He first appears almost as a footnote in 2 Samuel 4:4, where his story is a grim one. What do you learn about him?

b. The "news about Saul and Jonathan" referred to here is
their death. Upon the death of the king and his eldest
son, there was a struggle for power, despite the fact that
David had already been anointed king (1 Samuel 16).
When Saul had acted contrary to God's commands and
then tried to justify his actions, what had Samuel told
him (1 Samuel 13:13–14)?

c. In this struggle for control, what happened to Saul's son
Ish-bosheth, Mephibosheth's uncle (2 Samuel 4:5–8)?

So, as Saul's descendant who could claim the throne, Mephibosheth has much to fear, but having been crippled during
an attempt to flee the violence, he has no way to defend himself. In fact, my Bible's footnote tells me his name had been
changed from Meribaal (opponent of Baal) to Mephibosheth,
which means "from the mouth of the shameful thing." How's
that for a name that makes you feel loved and inspires confidence?

Mephibosheth's story resumes a few chapters (but several
years) later, after David's kingship has been firmly established.
Mephibosheth was five when Saul died (2 Samuel 4:4), and now
we see that he has a son of his own (2 Samuel 9:12). Read the
rest of his story in 2 Samuel 9:1–13.

5a. When David has firmly established his throne, what
question does he ask (2 Samuel 9:1)?

• • •

b. In making this request, David wants to fulfill a promise he made decades earlier to his best friend, Saul's son Jonathan. This promise is found in 1 Samuel 20:15. What covenant does David make with Jonathan?

c. But Mephibosheth, who has been in hiding for years, has no way of knowing this. What are we told in 2 Samuel 9:5?

The word used for "sent" and "brought" is *laqach*. It is translated "fetched" in the KJV, but in addition has the meaning of "to carry away, to seize." There would be no reason for Mephibosheth not to believe that his would be the next head literally on the chopping block. And I can only imagine that Mephibosheth's response in 2 Samuel 9:6 is not so much bowing in honor but rather lying flat on the ground begging the king for mercy.

6a. What are David's first words to him (2 Samuel 9:7)?

b. Then he spells out the rest of the reason for bringing Mephibosheth here. What does he say?

c. What is Mephibosheth's response (2 Samuel 9:8)?

Mephibosheth's response is not false humility. Rather, he knows the absolute contempt in which David could hold him. Notice how this phrase is used as one of contempt in 1 Samuel 17:43 and 2 Samuel 16:9.

e. But rather than kill him, the king restores him, returning to him that which once belonged to his grandfather Saul. Beyond that, what else does he decree (2 Samuel 9:10)?

f. And now, complete the phrase from 2 Samuel 9:11: "So Mephibosheth ate at David's table, like _____."

In the ancient Middle East, covenants were often concluded with a shared meal, which expressed a bond of friendship between two parties. Here, it was more than just friendship: David was welcoming his former would-be enemy into his household and declaring him family. Read David's words to God in Psalm 23:5–6, which easily could have been the words of Mephibosheth.

When I look at their stories, I realize that we, too, are Zacchaeus and Mephibosheth. Like Zacchaeus, we might feel that we are separated from the King because of what we have done. (Notice what Zacchaeus was called in Luke 19:7.) And yet, the King says, "I want to come to your home today."

• • •

7a. How does He say the same to us in Revelation 3:20?

   b. Like Mephibosheth, we may feel unworthy to come into the presence of the king because of our past or our family history. What does 2 Samuel 9:13 remind us about Mephibosheth?

   c. Yes, we know—if it's about an invitation to the feast, to be in the presence of the King, we don't have a leg to stand on. Except grace. Except God. Every day when we look in the mirror, we are reminded that we are sinful and unclean, and no matter how beautifully we clothe ourselves, what are we reminded in Isaiah 64:6?

   d. Our King invites us to come to the table with Him not because of who we are, but because of whose we are— His beloved. What are we reminded in Song of Songs 2:4?

The enemy wants us to believe that we are "less than" and not worthy. He wants to remind us of all the ways we fall short. When he places doubts, we do not see ourselves as of any value. But God's love for us goes further than knocking at our door, further than inviting us to the banquet table.

● ● ●

8a. What are the words of 1 John 3:1?

_____

_____

_____

_____

_____

God's words here remind us that we have value. He reminds us that nothing can separate us from His love. He reminds us that we are His beloved children. I like the way it is stated in the NIV: "See what great love the Father has lavished on us, that we should be called children of God! And that is what we are!"

    b. Take a minute to look up *lavish* in your dictionary. What do you notice?

My dictionary says, "extended, bestowed, or occurring in profusion; to extend or give in great amounts or without limits." It also tells me it's from an old French word meaning "downpour of rain," derived from *laver*, which means "to wash." John 3:16 uses the same word translated "lavished" in 1 John 3:1. God loved us so much that He poured out, lavished, His love upon us by giving us His one and only Son.

    c. How does Paul describe the whole event in Galatians 4:4–7?

The word translated "love" in 1 John 3:1 is *agape*, and literally it is a "love feast." God invites us to His "love feast," His banquet table, not merely as His guest, but also as His child.

● ● ●

9a. John 1:12 tells us more. How do we become God's children?

  b. Notice that membership in God's family is by grace alone. How does Ephesians 2:8 confirm this?

  c. Romans 8:17 calls us not just God's children but also His heirs. What gifts, rights, or abilities come along with that title? Read Romans 8:14–17. Which of these gifts, rights, or abilities resonates *most* with you?

Several things stand out to me. First, we need no longer be afraid because we have been more than just freed from slavery, we have been made sons and daughters. Second, because we are God's children, when we are afraid, we can cry out, "Abba Father." Someone once explained to me that this would be like crying out "Daddy!" As God's child, I can picture myself crawling up into His lap for security and a hug or just to hear Him tell me He loves me.

  d. When was the last time you "crawled up" into your Daddy God's lap and poured out your heart to Him? If you feel comfortable, share this with your group. If it's been awhile, maybe it's time.

Third, according to Romans 8:17, because I am God's child, I am also His heir, an heir to an inheritance that is not of this world.

• • •

10a. How does David describe the inheritance in Psalm 16:6?

b. How does Psalm 33:12 describe the people who are God's heritage ("inheritance" in NIV)?

c. And what is my response according to Psalm 106:5?

Oh, that I would delight in being called a child of God and know the joy of my inheritance! Zacchaeus knew the joy of a visit from the King. Mephibosheth delighted in sitting at table with King David. I experienced the joy of a royal parade. And we know the true joy to be found in being adopted as heirs and coheirs with Christ. Don't let the enemy tell you that you are unworthy. You are a child of the one true King!

Prayer of Reflection:

Dear God, You are not just the Creator of the universe
but also the King of my heart. Help me to remember
that I am Your child and heir to a delightful
inheritance. I rejoice in that life with You today.
In Jesus' name. Amen.

SESSION SEVEN

"MIRROR, MIRROR,
ON THE WALL . . ."

"For the LORD sees not as man sees: man looks on the
outward appearance, but the LORD looks on the heart."

1 Samuel 16:7b

How many different mirrors do you look at in a day? If you're like me, you may look in the bathroom mirror to style your hair and put in your contacts, a full-length mirror to check your outfit before you head out for the day, and perhaps a mirror by the door for one last quick check of your makeup. The house we just bought has a lighted magnifying mirror by my sink in the bathroom (the better to see all those unsightly chin hairs). Once I leave the house, there's the rearview mirror in my car, a mirror on the visor on the passenger side, and any number of mirrors in the places that I'm going. Does the image in the mirror match what you expect to see, or does your reflection betray you?

When my daughter was four, she wanted to be Ariel, the Disney version of *The Little Mermaid*, for Halloween. She told me so every day for months. So I made her a mermaid costume, with green lamé scales, a swishy tail, and a shell-shaped bag to gather candy. Since my daughter's hair is dark and curly, and Ariel's is straight and red, I bought her a long red wig to top off the costume. Every day while I was sewing it, she'd take a look, admire the costume, or show it off to a friend. She was going to be the best Little Mermaid ever.

On October 31, she donned the tail and the wig, gave me her best mermaid smile, and posed for some pictures. She was adorable. Then my husband came home from work, and rather than show him the costume, she slammed the door in his face. We had a "Trunk or Treat" costume festival at church that night, and I coaxed Brianna into the car, thinking that when she saw her friends, she would forget whatever was bothering her and get into the swim of things.

But when we got there, she didn't want to get out of the car. When she finally did, she hid behind me. And that's where she stayed the whole night. No one but me saw her in her full red-headed glory. Somewhere between the last photograph and my husband's hi-honey-I'm-home, Brianna lost all confidence in herself. I'm not sure what happened, except I think that when she caught a glimpse of herself in the mirror, her reflection didn't match the Disney animated character's. None of my words of assurance made a difference. Her image did not live up to her imagination.

I think I suffer from a similar mindset. Do you? Why is it so hard to look in the mirror and say, "I'm beautiful"? What is true beauty, anyway, and how do we attain it?

• • •

1. Although he is speaking in metaphor, how does Ezekiel warn of the danger of seeing oneself as beautiful in Ezekiel 28:17?

2a. Do we think it's wrong to see ourselves as beautiful, that no good will come from it? Looking to the Book of Esther, Queen Vashti was being displayed before the powerful visitors to her husband's kingdom as a sex object (Esther 1:11). She refused to be put on display, and what was the result (Esther 1:12, 18–19)?

b. As a result of Vashti's banishment, what search was made throughout the land (Esther 2:2–4)?

c. Who was among those taken in the search (Esther 2:8)? Notice the verb, *taken*. The word means "carried away"— not by choice.

d. What was the fate of the girls who were gathered (Esther 2:12–14)?

Now I have to confess that at first glance, I wouldn't take this as a great consequence. A year of beauty treatments— what's wrong with that? I've given at least passing thought to getting an extreme makeover. Passing thought, that is, until I had my first (and only) spa day. A facial, actually, as a gift from my husband.

Amanda walked me into a facial room and asked a few questions about my skin care regimen, concerns, and allergies. She turned on a steamer, and the room had that "just out of the shower" humidity that I love. Amanda started by giving me a foot massage. It felt great and worked to relax me. Then it was time for the facial. I'm not sure how many lotions, oils, and gels she applied, but each felt good. Some were warm and put me into a deeply rested state. Her fingers worked over my face and neck, relaxing my muscles, kneading away tension.

Then, without warning, the extraction began. If you've had a facial you know there's nothing delightful or relaxing about that. With some kind of tool of torture (I didn't ask to see what she used, but I cannot imagine thumbscrews being any more painful), she pushed and plucked at my face. "Surely this must end soon," I thought. "How much ugliness can there be?" Yet she kept pushing and plucking. Minutes seemed much longer until finally the torture ended.

Then Amanda gave me a complimentary waxing, removing hair from my lip and chin (I am aging, and not always gracefully). The stinging pain as the wax was ripped off was momentary but intense. Who knew true beauty could be so painful? After that, my desire for an extreme makeover passed.

● ● ●

3a. Now, you may regularly have facials and waxings and the like. And you're saying "Susan, get a life. It's not so bad." But remember, Esther was taken against her will (today we would call this kidnapping) and forced into a life in which the *only* thing that mattered was her beauty. Read verse 14 carefully. How many chances did the young girls have to please the king?

The "Miss Babylonia Beauty Pageant" could not help but end badly for 99 percent of the young women kidnapped, er, recruited. The ancient Jewish historian Josephus says four hundred women were selected. If they weren't pleasing enough or beautiful enough, they would be discarded, destined to a life in limbo, never to marry, knowing that their beauty was not enough and they were without value.

b. The pressure to be beautiful could be too great to bear, especially since we have internalized the first half of Proverbs 31:30. What does it say?

c. So, seeing ourselves as beautiful is often difficult in spite of—or because of—the multibillion dollar beauty industry. If beauty is only skin deep, take heart at the words of 1 Samuel 16:7. Write them here (this verse is also the Mirror Message for this lesson):

_____

_____

_____

_____

_____

4a. So, what indeed is it that makes us beautiful? For that
we look to 1 Peter 3:3–4. What are we told?

If beauty is only skin deep, then true beauty is something
deeper. True beauty comes not from what we put on and is not
reflected by what we see in the mirror; it is from within. The NIV
translation of 1 Peter 3:3 says, "Your beauty should not come
from outward adornment." In the ESV it reads, "Do not let your
adorning be external." Imagine my surprise when I discovered
the word for "adorning" in the Greek is *kosmos*, which also
translates "world."

Is your world centered around how you look? You don't
have to be a diva for this to be true. How much time do you
spend "putting on your face" in the morning? Do you get palpi-
tations at the thought of a quick run to the drug store at 11 p.m.
to get medicine for your sick child because you already took off
your makeup? I read of one woman who says even her husband
has never seen her without makeup.

b. While these may be extremes, how do you feel about
yourself without jewelry, styled hair, and the right ward-
robe? without cosmetics? (Even this English word is
from the same Greek root, *kosmos*.) Be honest.

Please don't misunderstand me. I'm not saying that we
should ignore our appearance (and I don't believe Peter is saying that either). I'm just saying it shouldn't become our world,
our primary concern.

Instead, where does the beauty come from, according to 1
Peter 3:4? The NIV says "your inner self," while the ESV says the

"hidden person of the heart." The heart that is not visible to the world, but visible only to God. The ESV goes on to call it "imperishable beauty." The Greek *apthartos* means "undecaying," no matter how much we age or wrinkle, no matter how gray our hair.

    c. As 1 Peter 3:4 concludes, what is this imperishable beauty?

I love the literal translation for "quiet spirit." *Hesuchios* means "keeping one's seat." For some reason this visual just makes me smile, and I wonder how many times I should keep my seat rather than become outraged or indignant at a perceived "injustice," like when someone cuts in front of me at the checkout.

    d. What about you—are you good at "keeping your seat"?

Who are some of these biblically beautiful women, who though perhaps fading on the outside, have a gentle and quiet spirit? Surely the widow of Zarephath was such a woman. Read her story in 1 Kings 17:8–24.

We know she is a widow, we know she is living in time of drought, and it's important to know that she was not an Israelite. In fact, she is from Sidon, the very heart of Baal worship, homeland to the wicked queen Jezebel, who soon will be seeking Elijah's death. The widow was down to her last cup of flour. Surely she was not a woman who had the time, energy, or wherewithal for outward adornment. Let's look a little closer and see wherein her beauty lies.

● ● ●

5a. What does the prophet ask in verse 10, and what does the widow begin to do in verse 11?

b. When Elijah next asks for a little bread, how does she respond (v. 12)?

c. Can you hear her despair? She's not just poor, she's destitute, literally down to her last meal. Yet her desperate heart recognizes something about this stranger. What are the first several words of 1 Kings 17:12?

Does she believe in this unknown God of the Israelites? I would guess the answer is "not yet." But she recognizes Him and calls Him a living God. Perhaps because of that declaration, the next words out of Elijah's mouth are "Don't be afraid," followed by the request to take that last bit of her meager supply of food and make him a meal.

I have never been asked to give up my last bite of food. Even if I had been, I would know that there would be another meal just around the corner. I did complete a twenty-four-hour meditative fast once, but even as I willingly skipped three meals, I knew that in twenty-four hours I would eat again. I imagine, however, that if I were asked for my last bit of bread, if in fact my family and I were starving, I would not *hesuchios*. I would not keep my seat. I would moan and groan and sputter and protest. Maybe, if I were extremely faith-filled at the moment, I might agree to share the bread.

● ● ●

d. How do you think you would respond? Or perhaps you have been in a desperate situation and identify with the widow. If so, please share your experience with your group.

Elijah doesn't ask her to share. She has one serving left that she's already going to have to split with her son, and Elijah commands, "Go make me a serving first."

e. She responds with a quiet and gentle spirit for a stranger who serves a strange but living God. What are we told in 1 Kings 17:15?

f. Verse 16 tells us what gift this beautiful woman received. Describe it here:

g. When the story doesn't end there, and the woman's son falls ill and dies, we witness the first instance of a person being raised from the dead recorded in Scripture (vv. 17–23). After the son is delivered back to his mother, alive, what declaration does this beautiful woman make (v. 24)?

The Shunammite woman was also biblically beautiful. Her story can be found in 2 Kings 4:8–37. This gentle woman has the gift of hospitality. When the prophet Elisha passes by her home, she offers—no, urges—him to eat bread. So whenever he passes her way, he stops to eat.

6a. Recognizing Elisha to be a holy man of God, what does she urge her husband to do?

b. In response to her hospitality, what offer does Elisha make (2 Kings 4:13)? And what is the woman's response?

This woman didn't make offers of kindness as bribes, expecting something in return. In fact, when Elisha makes an offer, she responds that she "*dwells* among her own people." In fact, the word she uses is *yashab*, and it means "to sit down in quiet." Remind you of a New Testament word? I can only wonder, if she had been a New Testament woman, would she have said "I am *hesuachios*"? In effect, this woman is saying, "I have a quiet spirit. I am content." And we might also infer she is beautiful.

Elisha learns that this woman is childless and her husband is old. When he dies, she could find herself destitute (children were a widow's only financial security in old age).

c. What is Elisha's promise through God (v. 16)? the woman's response?

I know from personal experience the heartbreak of being childless. I can imagine how long it must have taken for her to be able to say, "I am content." And I can well hear her response in my mind, "Please don't lie to me."

• • •

d. What happens (v. 17)?

This, however, is not the end of her story either, and I think the rest of the story shows the depth of her faith in the face of severe calamity.

    7a. Read verses 20 and 21. What happened to her son when he had grown (though the word used indicates that he is still a young man)?

      b. How does this beautiful woman respond? Note the details (vv. 21–23).

Two things stand out for me. First, she places her son on Elisha's bed, and second, she tells her husband "all is well." This reminds me of Jesus' words as recorded in Mark 5:39, several centuries in the future: "The child is not dead but sleeping." No doubt she had heard of Elijah and the widow of Zarephath. In telling her husband "all is well" ("it shall be well" in KJV), she expresses supreme confidence and faith that the God who gave her this child would also give her back her child. I am reminded of one Christian woman speaker who says, in the words of a classic hymn, "It may not be well with my circumstance, but 'It Is Well with My Soul.'"

This sorrowing mother didn't sit down passively and lament her son. And although she is filled with faith that God isn't done with him yet, still she raced to the prophet and fell at his feet. Don't mistake her anguish here as a lack of faith.

● ● ●

c. Compare 1 Kings 4:30 to Genesis 32:26. How are they similar?

While Jacob says, "I will not let you go unless you bless me," the Shunammite woman also refuses to let the prophet go, knowing that from his hands will come the blessing. Indeed, it is from God's hands that all blessings flow. Surely this beautiful woman recognized that. In the next several verses, Elisha returns to the woman's home.

d. Read 1 Kings 4:33. What does Elisha do?

e. He recognized, as we recognize, that it is not in his power to raise the dead to life, but it is in God's hands. And when, in fact, the boy sneezes and opens his eyes, how does the woman respond?

The Hebrew word *shachah* means "to prostrate oneself, especially in homage to God; to worship." The Shunammite woman's response is beautiful.

8. Lydia is a woman of beauty. Her New Testament account is briefly told in Acts 16:14–15, 40. Though she was a businesswoman, and perhaps wealthy, that's not the source of her beauty. What is?

We are reminded that beauty is not something we put on, not something we check in the mirror, but something that is within. I think of other biblical women: Elizabeth, the mother

• • •

of John the Baptist; Mary, the mother of Jesus; the woman with the bleeding sickness. These women and so many more found themselves relying on God, having faith in His word. They were, in a word, beautiful.

Returning to Peter's words in 1 Peter 3:4, true beauty is unfading, imperishable.

9. What does Paul tell us about perishable and imperishable things in 1 Corinthians 15:53?

10. What does Peter say in 1 Peter 1:18–23?

While outward things may perish, while physical beauty fades, wrinkles, or turns gray, true beauty does not. It comes from the inner confidence of salvation in Jesus Christ, who is Himself without blemish or defect. When we live and move and breathe in Him, we have a beauty that is unfading. When Jesus comes into your heart, He accomplishes the words of Isaiah 61:3.

And now, if you'll permit me, one more story: I'm overweight; my face is plain; my hair is straight, thin, and limp. When I look in the mirror, "beautiful" is far from what I see. Sometimes I don't recall thinking that of myself since my wedding day, despite my husband's declaration that I am.

But one night, at about the same time as our mermaid fiasco, my daughter decided to give me a new hairdo. She stood behind me holding a comb, a brush, and a spray bottle of water, with which she drowned my hair. When she returned from the bathroom with hair elastics, I braced myself for a "Brianna-do." When she was done, I looked in the mirror and saw a ponytail on the left side of my head, and most of the remaining hair falling out of a bun in the back. My hair was wet and tight to my head, and I couldn't wait for her to go to bed so I could remove the elastics and brush it out.

"Thanks for combing my hair, Brianna," I said, as much to model saying "thank you" as anything else. "You're welcome, Mommy," she responded, adding brightly, "You're beautiful."

It took a minute to sink in. I'm beautiful.

I am beautiful.

It's not the curves of my body or the complexion of my skin. It's not the thickness, curl, or color of my hair, but I'm beautiful. Not because the world calls me beautiful. Not even because my husband and daughter call me beautiful. I'm beautiful because *God* calls me beautiful. In the words of Psalm 45:11, "Let the king be enthralled by your beauty; honor him, for he is your lord" (NIV).

Prayer of Reflection:

O Father God, the desire of my heart is to be

beautiful, not as the world sees beauty but as You see

it. Because I am transformed in Christ, You see past

my outward appearance to my heart. Help me to

quiet my spirit and put my trust in You. In Jesus' name.

Amen.

• • •

SESSION EIGHT

FUN HOUSE
MIRRORS
AND POOPY
DIAPERS

MIRROR MESSAGE:

"Bless the LORD, O my soul, and forget not all His benefits,
who forgives all your iniquity, who heals all your diseases,
who redeems your life from the pit, who crowns you with
steadfast love and mercy." Psalm 103:2–4

R aise your hand if you like shopping. Keep it up if you like
clothes shopping. How about swimsuit shopping? You
may have raised your hand for the first question, but if your
size is hard to find, you may not have it up for the second. And
even the truly beautiful among us (although I venture to guess
that few of us see ourselves in this category) generally dislike
the third. I think that's because when we look at ourselves in

a swimsuit, it's as though we are looking in a fun house mirror and all our flaws are freakishly distorted. All we see is the ugly, the way our body doesn't measure up to the model on the magazine cover. Hips too big. Breasts too small. Muffin top and cellulite. Ugh. Ugly. We fall short; we don't make the grade.

I excelled in school. Good grades came easily to me, often without my even cracking a book. But making the grade as a parent wasn't so easy. Now I wanted to crack the books but could not find one to crack. No two authors seemed to agree on child-rearing, and no one was familiar with my two children and their individual quirks. I didn't solicit advice from friends because I don't like to admit that the things I am doing aren't working (besides, their children aren't my children either). Wherever I turned, I saw a distorted view of what I thought good parenting is. My parenting shortcomings seemed to converge the spring my oldest child, Matt, turned three and my parents came for an Easter visit.

I'm not a perfectionist, and I didn't come from a home where that was the standard. As the fourth of five children, I was used to seeing a home in disarray. We children weren't perfect (though I want to think that I was close [smile]). My mom is not a perfectionist either, but she is a rememberer. I married later (at age 31), and she had married early (at age 20), and for years as my birthday rolled around and I still wasn't even dating anyone, she would remind me, "When I was your age, I was married and had a child." "When I was your age, I was married and had two children." "When I was your age, I was. . . ." You get the picture. Now that I was married with two children, I finally felt like I had made the grade.

Now my parents were coming to visit, and the A-student in me wanted to display an A-family. To me, this meant children should behave perfectly, and three-year-olds should be potty trained. Well, my three-year-old wasn't behaving well or potty trained. Matt had an accident in the morning, and in the afternoon he hadn't napped long enough. We were all a little cranky, and maybe it was me who needed to nap. I can't remember what we were doing, but I noticed Matt was wet. Again. I raged, took him to the bathroom, pulled off his pants, and set him on the potty. As I did, I stepped barefooted right in (excuse my language) poop, just as he told me, "Mommy, I pooped." Got that, Matt! I can feel it!

But wait, there's more. Holy Week is busy at our house since my husband is the music minister at our church, and with Good Friday services at 6:00 and 7:30, and choir warm-ups at 5:30, my mom offered to cook an early dinner so we could get to church on time. Matt wouldn't eat a bite. Frustration that had been building all day erupted to the surface. I ranted, I raved, I tried to cajole, shame, and yes, even force Matt to eat. I picked up a bite of food and stuffed it in his mouth.

Who was this lunatic? My parents and my husband stared at me. In that moment, even I didn't know who I was. But I did know that I was failing as a mom. I left the table with a lump in my throat.

Alas, the day wasn't over. My husband left for church, and I set about getting myself and the kids ready to go. To worship. On Good Friday. As I got myself dressed, I noticed Matt, once again, was wet. I, once again, dragged him to the bathroom, pulled down his pants, and this time stuck my hand right in the . . . well, you know.

And I finally stopped. First I cried, then I laughed, then I cried again, as I asked Matt's forgiveness for getting so angry. And I asked God for forgiveness for putting appearances in place of feelings and love, for letting my feelings of inadequacy become intolerance, for not showing the love to my son that God had shown to me, and for driving the nails into the cross myself.

Our lives are filled with poopy places and not-so-fun house mirrors. Sin is front and center and overblown in our lives and distorts our view of ourselves and others. We don't measure up to our expectations for ourselves, let alone God's will for us, and we're afraid that God can never forgive us.

Jacob lived in that place of unforgiveness for years. Catch up on his story a bit in Genesis 27. You may remember that Jacob, whose name means "deceiver," tricked his blind father into giving Jacob his brother's blessing (Genesis 27:18–29). His brother, Esau, was, understandably, not happy with Jacob.

1a. What is his response in Genesis 27:41?

The word used here is emphatic: "Esau *hated* Jacob because of the blessing." The word in Hebrew is *satam*, which means "to lurk, persecute, hate, oppose oneself against." It is used only three times in the Bible. Not by accident I believe, it is nearly identical in form to the Hebrew word for "attack, accuse, adversary, resist"—the archenemy of good. That Hebrew word is *satan*. I believe that Esau was filled with Satan for his brother and said, "I'm gonna wait until just the right time, and then I will attack."

b. When Rebekah, the mother of these two feuding twins, hears of Esau's plotting, what does she do (Genesis 27:42–45)?

And so, Jacob leaves home, but not before his father Isaac again blesses him, passing along the blessing God made to Abraham and to Isaac. (See Genesis 28:3–4.)

● ● ●

2a. As he flees, he stops for the night to rest, and while he is resting, what does he dream (Genesis 28:12–15)?

b. Yes, in his dream, God confirms that Jacob is indeed the son on whom the promise rests. With what words does the dream end (Genesis 28:15)?

Fast-forward several chapters as Jacob arrives at his uncle's home, meets and falls in love with Rachel, works for seven years to get her hand in marriage, is deceived into marrying her sister Leah, then works for another seven years to receive Rachel's hand in marriage, begins his large family, and prospers his sheep. All the while, Jacob has been on the lam from his brother.

3. How long did Jacob remain at his uncle's home, according to Genesis 31:38?

Do you think that every day of that time Jacob was looking over his shoulder, fretful that his brother would come after him to seek revenge? I doubt it. He probably got caught up in his day-to-day life, and I imagine there were many days when he didn't think about Esau, or he hoped that it had all blown over and that his mother would send a message that he could come home (Genesis 27:45). But I also imagine that there were some days when he wondered if he would ever be forgiven, *could* he ever be forgiven? Living with unforgiveness is like that: you never know when the other shoe will drop.

But finally Jacob does know that it is time to return, to seek forgiveness. And it's not without trepidation that he plans his return, especially as he takes his family, gathers his sheep, and flees his father-in-law, fearing this man would never let him leave since he had so prospered him.

4a. When Jacob sends his servants before him to Esau with the message that he is returning, what do the servants return and tell him (Genesis 32:6)?

b. Describe Jacob's response (Genesis 32:7–12).

c. Yes, Jacob is filled with fear. He knows that Esau might still be holding a grudge, but what does he also know (vv. 9–12)?

He knows God, and he knows God's promises. And he is ready to rely on those promises. Sort of. Is it easy? No! Jacob still fears how Esau may react. Perhaps William Shakespeare said it best through Hamlet: "Conscience doth make cowards of us all." He decides to try to buy his brother's forgiveness, resting in what he can do rather than resting on God's word.

I can pack a lot in my minivan, but Jacob's family caravan is no match for Esau's four hundred men. His two hundred goats and two hundred ewes would not stand against an army of four hundred men who were intent to kill. His two wives, two female servants, and eleven children would be as nothing against the wrath of an angry, unforgiving brother.

● ● ●

d. And in fact, Jacob's actual meeting with Esau is rather anticlimactic. What is Esau's response when he finally comes face-to-face with Jacob (Genesis 33:1–11)?

Really, if we're going to talk about forgiveness, it's the tale of two brothers, and much of the trouble seems to come back to a stolen blessing.

5a. Take a moment to look back at that part of the story in Genesis 27. What did Isaac ask Esau to do, and why (Genesis 27:1–4)?

b. You can read the details, but know that Jacob deceives the blind Isaac into believing that he is his brother Esau. Summarize the blessing that Isaac gives Jacob (vv. 27–29).

When Esau finds out what has happened, he begs his father, "Have you not reserved a blessing for me?" (v. 36), and at last Esau receives a blessing too. Although it is perhaps not the blessing he wanted. I cannot help but wonder at the implications for verse 40, especially the second half of this verse.

c. What does it say?

While the NIV and ESV say, "when you grow *restless* . . . ," the KJV says, "when thou shalt have the *dominion*." The Hebrew word is *ruwd*, and it means both "to ramble" and "to have dominion, to be lord." I think, then, that both translations are good ones, but for our purposes today, I like the second. Think of it this way, as God is saying through Isaac, "You, Esau, are going to be ruled by anger, by unforgiveness, but when you decide to have dominion over it, to be lord over your own emotions rather than be ruled by them, then you will break this yoke from your neck."

    d. A yoke is often seen as an emblem of servitude, subjugation, and slavery. We can be bound to sin, slaves to unforgiveness, steered wherever our emotions take us, or we can take off that yoke. Jesus gives us another option. What is it, according to Matthew 11:28–30?

In fact, we can exchange one yoke for the other; we can hand over the burden of sin and unforgiveness to the One who has already died to remove that burden and exchange it for the easy yoke of uniting ourselves with Him. He will carry our burden and make it light. I believe at some time during the ensuing twenty years, Esau did just that.

Indeed, the family reunion of the two brothers after two decades of anger and unforgiveness is anticlimactic because the really important meeting took place the night before. Read carefully what happened the night before, when Jacob separates himself from everyone and everything he brought with him. The account is found in Genesis 32:22–32.

6a. In one short verse we are told the crux of the night. Summarize verse 24 here:

_____

_____

_____

_____

_____

First, notice that Jacob was alone. All of his family was on the other side of the brook; no one was around to distract him, no one else on whose strength he could rely. Most sources agree that the "man" Jacob wrestled was God Himself, as Jacob realizes in verse 30 (and confirmed in Hosea 12:3–4), God in the form of an angel, a preincarnation of Christ.

But what if Jacob's wrestling with God was a struggle over sin and forgiveness, over giving up our burdens to God, over deciding to go it alone or give it to God? Over even admitting to ourselves that we alone are not able.

b. John says it well in 1 John 1:8–9. Summarize what he says.

_____

_____

_____

_____

_____

What if God won't prevail over the sin until we give up the fight and submit ourselves to Him? What if we confess our sins and let them go and give them to God and receive the forgiveness that has already been won for us on the cross? And what if we wrestle with the sin and the need for forgiveness instead of resting in the Savior and receiving His blessing?

c. Finally, making Jacob stop the struggle, what does the man do (Genesis 32:25)?

Jacob realizes that he can fight no more; all he can do is hold on to God and ask for a blessing.

7a. Perhaps the blessing Jacob is looking for is the same one David would write about centuries later, in Psalm 32:1–2. Who is blessed according to this verse?

b. That is who we are: we are blessed. John says it too, in 1 John 2:12. We are the children he is talking about. Why are our sins forgiven?

c. Second Corinthians 5:19 also spells it out. How did God reconcile the world to Himself?

Reconcile is such a big "church word," but it really just means to bring into agreement or harmony, or even to exchange currency. When we get our bank statement, we reconcile our checkbook with the balance on the statement. Through Christ, God says, "Your sins don't count against you any more—I have brought them into balance. Through the death and resurrection of My Son, Jesus Christ, your sins are forgiven, the balance is zero. I am not counting your sins any more." (See Romans 4:8.)

● ● ●

In fact, to go back to Jacob's night alone, the night he wrestled, the crux of that night was the cross. And it is with our struggles too. Will we wrestle with God in prayer? Will we hold Him to His promises until He richly blesses us?

But even after letting go, we tend to pick it all up again. And so God wrenches our thigh; He gives us a soft spot (the Hebrew word for "thigh," *yarek*, means "to be soft") to remind us of what He's done for us. And I think that it's not by accident that in the Hebrew culture, promises were made by laying a hand under the thigh (see Genesis 24:2, 9; Genesis 47:29). As Christians, we, too, are crippled by our past. Our past haunts us and we sometimes have difficulty believing that Jesus really settled it, that He wants us to move on and trust Him.

8a. Is there an area of unforgiveness you are wrestling with? Something you don't believe God can forgive you for? Or someone you think you cannot forgive? Write it here. If you're not comfortable with that, write it in code. Or at least spend some time thinking about it if you are not comfortable writing or sharing it.

b. Guess what? When you confessed the sin with your mouth, the forgiveness is yours through the mouth of the pastor in Holy Absolution. What are God's words for us in Psalm 103:12?

I know that God is the God of time and of timing. I believe He allowed me to experience my "poopy day" on Good Friday precisely to serve as a reminder to me that no matter what place I find myself in, He has forgiven me through Christ's death on the cross. As Jesus' arms were spread east to west on the cross, as He took my sins upon His back on that Good Friday, the chains of sin that bound me were destroyed. My sins were removed from me as far as the east is from the west, and I now stand before God forgiven. His scarred hands are the proof of that forgiveness—for me, and for you as well.

Sometimes we need a reminder that God loves us despite our unworthiness. Jacob received a soft spot in his thigh, a physical reminder that his struggle with sin is overcome by the God who prevails. We receive reminders as well. Sometimes they are memories of poopy places that remind us that God has gone there and forgiven that. Sometimes they are Bible passages.

9. What reminder does God leave for us in each of the following passages?

    a. Isaiah 1:18

    b. Isaiah 43:25

    c. Micah 7:18–20

I especially like the end of Micah 7:18, where God reminds me that He delights to show mercy, He delights in steadfast love. What a relief. It's not a burden to Him—it's a *delight*! It's as if we are looking in a distorted fun house mirror when we allow our memories of our sinfulness to become larger than God's love. There's no truth in believing that we can sin bigger than God has already forgiven.

• • •

10. How does Paul say it in 1 Timothy 1:15–16?

When I think about that Good Friday so many years ago, I like the words of Psalm 40:2:

> He *drew me out of the pit of destruction,*
> *out of the miry bog;*
> *and set my feet upon a rock*
> *making my steps secure.*

Today and every day, when you look in the mirror, remember the words of Psalm 103:2–4. They were printed at the beginning of the lesson, but write them again here and on your heart.

_____

_____

_____

_____

• • •

Prayer of Reflection:

O Jesus, lover of my soul, You have already borne
the burden of all my sins and taken them to the cross.
Help me daily to turn my burdens over to You and
to live in forgiveness and peace. Amen.

Answer Guide

Session 1: Knowing the Person You See in the Mirror

1. Answers will vary.

2. Jacob's name means "deceiver." In order to get the blessing meant for the firstborn, his brother Esau, Jacob dressed in Esau's clothing, covered his smooth skin with goatskin, and pretended to his blind father to be his hairy brother. The trick works, his father is deceived, and Jacob gets the blessing.

3. We weren't redeemed with gold or silver, but with the precious blood of Christ.

4. "Called" or "summoned" could also be translated "chosen" or "selected." It's not a random calling but a purposeful one. God chose us out of all the people on the earth not because of anything we have done, but simply out of love. He loves us!

5. Sarah calls herself worn out and old. Gideon calls himself the weakest and least. But God calls Gideon "mighty man of valor."

6. The second half of Genesis 1:2 says that "the Spirit of God was hovering over the face of the waters." We get our new name from God's mouth . . . from the Spirit of God.

7. God told Adam to name the animals, and whatever you call them, that is its name. Once called by the name, that is who or what it is.

9. Abram is renamed Abraham, which means the father of a multitude. Jacob is renamed Israel, which means he struggles with God. In Psalm 73, we are told that "it is good to be near God." (And it is, even if you are wrestling with Him!) In 2 Corinthians 12:9–10, Paul says he will boast all the more gladly in his weaknesses so that the power of God may rest upon him.

10. Mark 2 and Luke 5 both tell the story of Jesus calling Levi, the tax collector. In Matthew, we learn that Levi is also known as Matthew. Tax collectors were Jewish locals employed by Romans (yuck) to collect taxes (double yuck). They could collect as much as they wanted and keep the excess (triple yuck). They were hated by the Jews and considered traitors.

SESSION 2: CHOSEN

1–2. God doesn't look at appearance or stature. God looks at the heart! In 1 Samuel 16:12, David is called "ruddy" (having a fresh, healthy look; a "pretty boy"). In verse 18, we learn he is a skillful musician, a brave warrior, a wise speaker, and good looking. We learn in 1 Samuel 17:50 that he has a good aim—he kills Goliath with a stone. And finally, 1 Samuel 18:14 tells us he had success in all he did.

3. God calls David a man after God's own heart. God chose the nation of Israel not because of their greatness but because of His love.

4. Matthew was a tax collector, sneered at by Pharisees, grouped with "sinners."

• • •

5. Levi (Matthew) got up, left everything, and followed Jesus. Then he threw a party and invited his tax collector friends. Jesus doesn't choose the healthy for His team, but the sick. Not the righteous, but sinners. In Romans 5:8, we are told "that while we were still sinners, Christ died for us."

6. Aaron performs signs (miracles). His staff became a snake; he raised his staff and the river flowed with blood.

7. Seventy elders of Israel went with Moses and Aaron to the mountain. There they saw God and ate and drank. And they promise that everything the Lord said, they will do.

8. Moses tells the elders to wait here with Aaron and Hur. If you have any problems, go to them. God had a garment made, a sacred garment to give him dignity and honor. And He gave him the Urim and Thummim to rest over his heart so he could always have a means for making decisions.

9. Aaron asks for all the gold earrings to be brought to him, and then he fashions them into an idol in the shape of a calf and builds an altar in front of it. When the people see the calf, they say, "These are your gods, O Israel, who brought you up out of the land of Egypt."

10. Aaron responds to Moses' question by blaming the people, saying they told him to make a god and that he threw the gold in the fire and it came out a cow. Fortunately, God tells Aaron and us that He is a compassionate God, "slow to anger, and abounding in love and faithfulness," and that He forgives and consecrates him for service.

11. Aaron and Miriam speak against Moses and his calling by God. God gives Miriam leprosy. Later, Aaron and Moses plead for mercy. Aaron stands between God and the people God would punish. Later, God tells Moses and Aaron that because they did not trust Him, they would not get to lead the people into the Promised Land. In 1 Corinthians, God says He chose the foolish, the weak, the lowly, the despised, the things that are not, so that no one can boast in their own goodness, strength, and ability.

SESSION 3: MORE THAN MEETS THE EYE

1. God tells the people to settle down: build houses, plant gardens, marry, have children—increase, don't decrease. Jeremiah's response to the prophet Hananiah's prophecy is "Yay! If it comes true." But he says the prophet who prophesies peace is sent by God only if the prophecy comes true. Two years later, he says, "The Lord didn't send you. You have persuaded the people to believe lies, and in less than a year, you will die because you have preached rebellion." The proof is in the pudding: two years later, Hananiah dies. By telling them to marry, have children, and so on, God is telling them they'll be there a while; they should plan on it.

2. God tells His people to seek the welfare of the place He has taken them and to pray for peace.

3. God promises after seventy years that He will come and keep His promise and bring His people back home. Joshua says not one of the promises the Lord has made has failed; every one has been fulfilled!

4. In Isaiah, God says He makes known "the end from the beginning." (In other words, before it began, God knew how it would all end.) In Revelation, He says He is the beginning and the end.

5. My thoughts on the Latin *texere* and the Sanskrit *tekton*: The carpenter, Jesus, has woven the textures in your life so that you can more clearly see and reflect Him!

6. In John, we are told that we will have tribulation in the world, but that Jesus has overcome the world. James says we are to consider our trials pure joy, because they develop perseverance in us, which is necessary to make us complete. And in Philippians, Paul tells us "that He who began a good work in [us] will bring it to completion at the day of Jesus Christ."

7. In Ecclesiastes, we hear that a cord of three strands is not easily broken. God is the third strand we wrap our lives around.

8. In Jeremiah 29:12, the Lord says that when we call upon Him, He will hear us. In this verse, God has allowed His people to endure decades of chastisement, which motivated their change of heart.

9. In Deuteronomy 4:29, God says that from there (wherever your "there" is) you will seek the Lord, and if you seek Him earnestly and with your whole heart, then you will find Him. In 2 Chronicles 15:3–4, we find out that for a long time, Israel had no priests to teach them, but in "their distress they turned to the LORD . . . and sought Him," and it was only then that they found Him. In fact, in 2 Chronicles 16, we read that the Lord continuously looks for people who are fully committed to Him so He can strengthen them. Not only will we find God if we seek Him, but He assures us that He is searching out those who seek Him!

Session 4: Bits and Pieces and a Kaleidoscope

1. Side by side in Genesis 37:3–4, we see Joseph's father's great love for him and his brothers' hate.

2. Joseph's dreams imply that his brothers will one day bow down to him. As a result, his brothers hate him all the more, and his father keeps quiet. When Jacob deceived his brother, Esau held a grudge and vowed one day to kill his brother.

3. Joseph's brothers plot to kill him and say that a vicious animal devoured him. Instead, they throw him into a well, and when traders come along, they sell him. Then they get Joseph's robe, slaughter a goat, and put the blood on the robe. When they show it to Jacob, he believes that a beast has killed his son. (In a sense, that's true: it's a beast of greed and envy!) In Genesis 39, Joseph flees the advances of his master's wife and leaves his robe behind. She uses the robe as evidence that Joseph tried to rape her.

4. In Genesis 39:21, however, we are told that "the Lord was with Joseph and showed him steadfast love and gave him favor." In his letter to Timothy, Paul says that despite the evil in his life, all the bad things he has done as well as what has been done to him, God has poured out His grace and favor through Jesus Christ.

6. Lazarus's sisters send word to Jesus that Lazarus "whom He loves" is sick. Despite that, Jesus stays two more days before coming to them.

7. Both Mary and Martha say, "If You had been here, my brother would not have died." They say it with the assurance that God the Son can do the impossible.

8. Answers will vary.

● ● ●

9. What brings glory to God? In Matthew, it is seeing people being healed. In Luke, it was the leper seeing that he himself was healed. Mark says that when Jesus heals the sins of the paralytic (which only God can do), the teachers are outraged, but when He heals the man, the people are amazed and bring glory to God. In John, when the people see what Jesus does for Lazarus, they put their faith in Him, in essence bringing praise and glory to God! But even before Lazarus is raised, Martha makes a confession that Jesus is the Christ, the Son of God, come to save the world.

10. How about a few more places where God is glorified? In Matthew 5:16, when our light shines and other people see our good deeds and praise God. In 1 Peter, whenever we speak or serve and do it in such a way that God will be praised. In John 12:16–17, after Lazarus is raised, the people continue to speak about it, spreading the word and bringing praise to God.

SESSION 5: A SERVANT'S HEART

1. In Matthew 20:26, God says whoever wants to be great must be a servant.

2. The events of 2 Samuel 11 take place in the spring, when kings go off to war.

3. In Exodus 4:12, God tells Moses "Now therefore go, and I will be with your mouth and teach you what you shall speak." When Paul begs for his "thorn" to be removed, God says, "My grace is sufficient for you, for My power is made perfect in your weakness." After still more complaints from Moses, God says to him, "Who gives man a mouth, or hearing, or sight?" In other words, don't you think I know how well you can speak?

4.   Martha is a doer. And she is distracted by all the prepa-
     rations that needed to be done; that is, Martha was *busy*!
     Jesus tells her she is worried about a lot of stuff that
     needs to be done, but really only *one* thing is needed.

5.   Moses prays that God would establish the works of his
     hands. In other words, his prayer is that God would show
     us what we *really* need to do. Your prayer may be some-
     thing like this: Dear God, delight in me. Grant me grace as
     I order my schedule today, and direct me toward the tasks
     You want me to do. Keep me ever mindful of Your direc-
     tion for my life. (But don't copy my prayer; really think
     about how Moses' words would fit your life.)

6.   You are to love our Lord God "with all your heart and
     with all your soul and with all your mind and with all your
     strength." In other words—fully, completely, and with
     everything we have!

7.   In 2 Corinthians 1:4, God reminds us that He comforts
     us in our troubles so that we might comfort others in the
     same way we have been comforted. We are to use our
     painful experiences to help others.

8.   Ehud was left-handed. While this is often seen as an an-
     noyance for those of you who are, it gave Ehud a special
     advantage for a surprise attack. Tabitha (also known as
     Dorcas) sewed clothes for the widows and the poor.

9.   First Peter 4:10 tells us to use our gifts to serve others, to
     be good stewards of God's grace in its various forms.

10. Ephesians 5 says we are to be imitators of God by living a
     life of love and service as a fragrant sacrifice to God. Just
     as our other giving should not be "reluctant" or "under
     compulsion," neither should be our service to others.

Session 6: Royalty

1. Zacchaeus climbed a tree.

2. Jesus stopped and saw Zacchaeus. He then called him out of the tree. He said, "I must stay at your house today."

3. Zacchaeus came down at once and welcomed Jesus gladly to his home. Then he gave half of his possessions to the poor, and he said that if he cheated anyone, he would give it back fourfold. Jesus recognizes Zacchaeus's belief in Him, and He tells him he has salvation just as Abraham had.

4. Mephibosheth is the son of Jonathan, the grandson of Saul. He was five years old when his father and grandfather were killed. While trying to flee with him, his nurse dropped him. Consequently, he was lame in both feet. Earlier, Samuel had told Saul that since he acted foolishly and didn't do as God commanded, his kingship would not endure. (If he had followed God's commands and acted wisely, God would have established his kingship over Israel for all time.) Ish-bosheth, Mephibosheth's uncle, was killed by David's people, and his head was brought to David in victory.

5. David asks if there is anyone left in Saul's family to whom he could show kindness because of his love for Jonathan. Decades earlier, he had made a covenant with Jonathan to never cut off his kindness from Jonathan's family. In 2 Samuel 9:5, we are told that David had Mephibosheth brought to him.

6. David says, "Don't be afraid." He says he brought Mephibosheth there to show him kindness for his father's sake. He says he's going to restore his land and give him a place at his table. Mephibosheth is astonished that David would even recognize a "dead dog" like him. Once he restores Mephibosheth to his table, he also decrees that Saul's servants are forever to farm the family farm and always to provide for Mephibosheth.

7. In Revelation, Jesus tells us that He is standing at the door of our hearts, knocking. He says, "Open the door and welcome Me and I will eat with you." Second Samuel reminds us that Mephibosheth ate at David's table despite the fact that he had crippled feet. In Isaiah, we are reminded that all our righteous acts are like a "polluted garment," but in the Song of Solomon we see that He takes us to the banquet feast because His banner over us is love.

8. In fact, God loves us so much that He calls us His children in 1 John 3:1. In Galatians 4, Paul says at just the right time God sent His Son to be our kinsman-redeemer, giving us full rights as sons (and daughters). We are no longer slaves, but we can call Him Father (or Dad!).

9. John 1:12 tells us that we become God's children when we receive Him and believe in His name. Ephesians reminds us that it is by grace we have been saved, through faith, solely as a gift from God. When Romans 8 reminds us that being children means being heirs, He says we receive the right not to fear, the right to call God "Father," and the knowledge that we are coheirs to an inheritance (not just the leftovers). However, to share in the glory we must also share in the suffering.

10. In Psalm 16, David says the inheritance is pleasant, delightful, and beautiful. In Psalm 33, the people of the heritage are blessed. My response, according to Psalm 106, is to enjoy the times when things are going well, share in the joy, and join with the other people of God in praising Him!

SESSION 7: "MIRROR, MIRROR, ON THE WALL . . ."

1. Ezekiel warns that with beauty comes pride.

2. When Vashti refused to be seen as a sex object, her husband became furious, and Vashti was never again allowed in the king's presence, lest other women think they could talk to their husbands in the same way. As a result, a search was made throughout the land for the most beautiful virgin who could please the king and become the new queen. Esther was taken in the search. Her fate was twelve months of beauty treatments.

3. Young girls had just one chance to please the king, one night. Proverbs 31 says that "charm is deceitful, and beauty is vain."

4. So what makes us beautiful? Peter says our beauty doesn't come from the outside, from hair, makeup, jewelry, or clothing, but from the inside, from a quiet and gentle spirit.

5. The prophet asks the widow to get him some water. She begins to do so. When he asks for bread, she says she barely has enough to provide one last meal for herself and her son before they lay down and die. Yet she recognizes something in the stranger, saying, "As the LORD your God lives . . . ," so she does what Elijah asks, and there was food for her and her son every day. The flour wasn't used up and the jug didn't run dry. In response, she gives a beautiful declaration of faith, "Now I know that you are a man of God, and that the word of the LORD in your mouth is truth."

6. The Shunammite woman urges her husband to build a guest room for Elisha. Elisha asks what he can do to repay her, but she answers that she is content. Through God, Elisha promises that by this time next year she will have a son. Her response could be stated, "Don't mess with me!" But in fact she does become pregnant and have a son.

7. Years later, the son has a severe headache and dies. His mother lays him on Elisha's bed, and then, as if nothing were wrong, goes to find Elisha. Like Jacob, this woman clings to the prophet, saying, "I know you have the power to bless me. Bless me! I won't let go until you do." When Elisha returns with her, he goes into the room, closes the door, and prays to the Lord. When her son sneezes, she falls at Elisha's feet, acknowledging the favor of God just granted her through the prophet.

8. Lydia is an encourager. She opened her house to the new "followers of the Way," was baptized along with her household, and welcomed other believers into her home.

9. Paul says "this perishable body must put on the imperishable."

10. Peter says that gold and silver (stuff) don't save us, only the precious blood of the Lord Jesus Christ, the Lamb without blemish, saves us.

Session 8: Fun House Mirrors and Poopy Diapers

1. Esau held a grudge and vowed that one day he would kill his brother. Rebekah tells Jacob to flee and to stay gone until Esau's anger subsides. She sends him to her brother Laban's house.

2. Fleeing, Jacob dreams of a stairway to heaven, and the Lord repeating the promise He made to Abraham, that one day we will have the land, and all the people of the earth will be blessed through him. At the end of the dream, God promises that He will not leave Jacob until He has done what He has promised.

3. Jacob remains at his uncle's for twenty years.

4. Jacob's servants tell him that his brother is coming to meet him with four hundred men. Jacob is fearful and distressed! He divides his people into two groups, hoping that at least one group will survive. And then he prayed, "Save me! Keep Your promise." Jacob knows God. He knows repentance. He knows prayer. And he knows the promise God made to him. When he finally meets Esau face-to-face, Esau tells him he can keep his stuff, as he (Esau) has plenty of his own.

5.   Isaac told Esau to kill a wild animal and prepare a meal
      for his father so that he could give his son his blessing
      before he died. The blessing of Isaac is that God would
      bless his son, prosper him, and that people would serve
      him and even his brother would bow down to him. (Re-
      member, Isaac thought he was blessing Esau. He recog-
      nized the rivalry between the brothers, and probably even
      that Jacob acted superior to his brother.) When he finally
      blesses Esau, he says, "When you grow restless, you will
      throw the yoke from your back." Jesus says, "Come to Me
      with your burdens, and take My yoke upon you, and I will
      give you rest."

6a.   John says if we say we are without sin, we are a Jacob,
      a deceiver. But if we confess our sins, we are forgiven,
      restored. To end the struggle, the man touches Jacob's hip
      socket, and Jacob's hip is wrenched.

6b.   Answers may vary, but should describe the scene where
      Jacob is alone and a man (God) engages in a physical
      altercation with him.

7.   Psalm 32:1–2 tells us that blessed is the one whose sins
      are "covered." God declares us "not guilty." According to
      1 John 2:12, our "sins are forgiven for His name's sake."
      And in 2 Corinthians 5:19, God says in Christ, He rec-
      onciles "the world to Himself, not counting their sins
      against them."

8.   "As far as the east is from the west," that's how far God
      has removed our transgressions from us!

9.   In Isaiah 1:18, God reminds us that though our "sins are
      like scarlet they shall be as white as snow." In Isaiah 43,
      He says He erases our sins for His own sake and elimi-
      nates them from His memory. And Micah 7 tells us that
      God is delighted to show us mercy!